CONFRONTING THE DEATH PENALTY

OXFORD STUDIES IN LANGUAGE AND LAW

Oxford Studies in Language and Law includes scholarly analyses and descriptions of language evidence in civil and criminal law cases as well as language issues arising in the area of statutes, statutory interpretation, courtroom discourse, jury instructions, and historical changes in legal language.

Series Editor:

Janet Ainsworth, *Seattle University School of Law*
Lawrence Solan, *Brooklyn Law School*

Editorial Board:

Janet Cotterill, *Cardiff University, UK*
Christopher Heffer, *Cardiff University, UK*
Robert Leonard, *Hofstra University*
Anne Lise Kjær, *University of Copenhagen*
Gregory Matoesian, *University of Illinois at Chicago*
Elizabeth Mertz, *University of Wisconsin Law School and American Bar Foundation*
Roger W. Shuy, *Georgetown University*

Law at Work: Studies in Legal Ethnomethods
Edited by Baudouin Dupret, Michael Lynch, and Tim Berard

Speaking of Language and Law: Conversations on the Work of Peter Tiersma
Edited by Lawrence M. Solan, Janet Ainsworth, and Roger W. Shuy

Discursive Constructions of Consent in the Legal Process
Edited by Susan Ehrlich, Diana Eades and Janet Ainsworth

From Truth to Technique at Trial: A Discursive History of Advocacy Advice Texts
Philip Gaines

Discourse, Identity, and Social Change in the Marriage Equality Debates
Karen Tracy

Translating the Social World for Law: Linguistic Tools for a New Legal Realism
Edited by Elizabeth Mertz, William K. Ford, and Gregory Matoesian

Conceptions in the Code: How Metaphors Explain Legal Challenges in Digital Times
Stefan Larsson

Deceptive Ambiguity by Police and Prosecutors
Roger Shuy

Legal Integration and Language Diversity: Rethinking Translation in EU Lawmaking
C.J.W. Baaij

Legal Translation Outsourced
Juliette R. Scott

Shallow Equality and Symbolic Jurisprudence in Multilingual Legal Order
Janny H.C. Leung

Strategic Indeterminacy in the Law: Linguistic Tools for New Legal Realism
David Lanius

Confronting
the Death Penalty

*How Language Influences Jurors
in Capital Cases*

ROBIN CONLEY RINER

OXFORD
UNIVERSITY PRESS

OXFORD

UNIVERSITY PRESS

Oxford University Press is a department of the University of Oxford. It furthers
the University's objective of excellence in research, scholarship, and education
by publishing worldwide. Oxford is a registered trade mark of Oxford University
Press in the UK and certain other countries.

Published in the United States of America by Oxford University Press
198 Madison Avenue, New York, NY 10016, United States of America.

© Oxford University Press 2016

First issued as an Oxford University Press paperback, 2020

This work was previously published under the name Robin Conley.

Library of Congress Cataloging-in-Publication Data
Conley, Robin, author.
Confronting the death penalty : how language influences jurors
in capital cases / Robin Conley.
p.   cm. — (Oxford studies in language and law)
Includes bibliographical references and index.
ISBN 978-0-19-933416-2 (hardcover) | ISBN 978-0-19-754554-6 (paperback)
1. Capital punishment—United States. 2. Jury—United States. 3. Decision
making. I. Title.
KF9227.C2C65 2016
345.73'0773—dc23
2015009933

To my parents,
for introducing me to language.

CONTENTS

ACKNOWLEDGMENTS

This book and the research behind it are, as I'm sure any author would acknowledge, very dear to me. Those who have helped it along its way are dear to me as well. The first thanks are due to my parents for making me into the person and, in the case of my father, the scholar that I am. Their support of my schooling, research, and writing has made this book and so much else possible. I would also like to recognize Steve Riner for his warm love and support and for the all-important laughter he brings to my life.

The research for this book was funded generously by grants from the Wenner Gren Foundation and the National Institute of Justice. The time I spent in Texas was made possible by their support, as well as by grants from the UCLA Department of Anthropology. My advisors and friends at UCLA have enriched my research and academic life more generally. I thank Alessandro Duranti, Justin Richland, Elinor Ochs, Candy Goodwin, and John Heritage for their continued advice, encouragement, and criticism. Because of them, I am miles from the first-year graduate student I was years ago. I also owe Paige Sullivan, Steve Black, and Netta Avineri my gratitude for reading drafts of the book as they progressed and my wonderful research assistant, Maria Orsini, for her swift and thorough work. I am additionally indebted to Bryan D. Carnes for his close reading of the many iterations of my chapters.

I am also grateful to and humbled by the people in Texas who allowed me into their lives. The attorneys, staff, and interns at the Texas Defender Service were a constant inspiration to me, and their support and friendship have been invaluable. They were the only organization brave enough to let an anthropologist in their midst, and I thank them for that. I would especially like to acknowledge Gwen Nolan, John Niland, Kathryn Kase, Peter Walker, Jared Tyler, Gloria Flores, and Alma Lagarda, from whom I learned so much. To the other attorneys who shared their practice, struggles, and triumphs with me, especially Billy Carter and Hope Knight, I hope I've done you justice. Also, Megan Fenner, your hospitality made my stay in Texas homey and safe, and I thank you for that. I must also acknowledge the defendants, victims, and families involved in Texas capital trials, whose pain permeated my days in Texas. The system is broken and its workings break everyone caught up in it.

And a final, resounding thank you to the capital jurors who were generous enough to lend me their time and stories. I hope I have treated your words well.

CONFRONTING THE DEATH PENALTY

1

Introduction:

"That's the hardest thing
I've ever had to do"

THE MAJORITY OF MY TIME in Texas was spent with words. Hearing that I was a linguistic anthropologist, death penalty defense attorneys continually thrust papers at me, asking whether their proposed jury instructions were comprehensible and how they might be interpreted. They sought my advice (wisely or not) on how best to phrase their closing arguments, and what to make of the potential juror who spoke reverently of his uncle, the police officer, during voir dire. When I spoke with capital jurors after their trials, we marveled at the complex verbiage of their instructions and how confused they were by legal jargon and the laws they were charged with interpreting. Even the Texas Prison Museum prominently displayed the last words of those who had been executed, exhibited next to printed menus of their final meals.

In my memories of fieldwork, this torrent of words is broken by poignant, wordless moments. I am taken back to the small room where I sat with a defense attorney while he restlessly waited to hear the fate of his client. He took my laptop from me and browsed through my playlist, settling on *Carmina Burana*. He sang along, his operatic tenor a surprising, pleasant break from the otherwise tense silence. I can still hear the sounds of shackles as a death row inmate approached the prison visiting room from somewhere down the inner hallway. I could always hear the inmates first, well before the hefty door swung open to reveal them standing in prison whites, flanked by guards. My nose seems to contain remnants of the stench from inside one of the oldest occupied prisons in Texas, body odor mixed with urine and old food. I recall sitting in a restaurant with a man who had served on a capital jury years before. The defendant he sentenced to death had recently been executed. The man cried briefly in that restaurant, attempting to process his role in another human's death. I can visualize a defendant's arm stretched out to me in a courtroom, strikingly pale from his time in prison, as he explained how he engineered a needle and tattooed himself while inside.

Texas capital jurors had similarly disjointed experiences. They too operated in a world of words—any legal trial takes human conflicts and textualizes them, reducing complex social interactions to verbal and written form (Felstiner, Abel, and Sarat 1980–81). From the start of jury selection, jurors were required to interpret arcane, complicated legal instructions and rules. During their deliberations, they had to somehow filter weeks of sitting through trials into a decision that could be reconciled with these rules.

Jurors' days in court, however, were also filled with affecting encounters that stood apart from the legal language they were usually occupied with. One juror spoke of the intense disgust that overtook him when he watched the defendant during trial. He was so sickened that he had to force himself not to look at the defendant any longer in order to try to remain fair, he explained. Another juror stammered as she recalled envisioning herself as the murder victim in her trial. The victim must have realized at some point, the juror figured, after being stabbed over fifty times, that she was not going to escape. A third juror spoke of her discomfort being seated in the courtroom next to the witness stand. She was physically anxious, she said, when cuffed inmates were brought next to her to sit and testify.

While, like mine, jurors' dealings with legal words were entwined with these stirring encounters, their processing of these experiences was highly restricted in comparison to my own. For one, I was able to see each crime and each trial from multiple perspectives, spending time in the courthouse watching testimony and later visiting crime scene locations, trying to visualize, for example, how an escaping inmate's truck careened into a prison guard on horseback, sending her flying to her death. I stood in the death house, gazing at the gurney where the defendants I shared courtroom space with every day would later take their last breaths. Jurors are not afforded such experiences. Their knowledge of crimes and defendants is limited to what is presented to them during trial, to attorneys' selective show-and-tell.

And despite the varied kinds of experiences capital jurors do have during trials, their last duty is one of words. Their emotional reactions and empathic imaginings must be molded to answer two cryptic questions on their jury charge—Will the defendant be a future danger? Does any evidence mitigate the defendant's blameworthiness?[1]—which translate trial encounters

---

1. Texas capital jurors' instructions, including these "special issue" questions, will be explained in depth in chapter 2.

into a language dictated by the law. Institutionally, this is when jurors' responsibilities end. Where these legal words lead—to the ultimate taking of a human life—is officially no longer their concern. But for many, they live and relive these words, these images, these emotions, recognizing the precise consequences their words have had.

• • •

That's the hardest thing I've ever had to do, to look at a man and, you know, know that I'm saying, you know, I don't think you should live.

I've always felt that the death penalty you know, was a good thing? This process here is kinda, makes you wanna, makes me wanna think about it . . . I, it's like I say, that's the hardest thing I ever had to do. And I never thought that it would be that hard.

— TWO FORMER TEXAS CAPITAL JURORS

This book asks one essential question: how can human beings sentence another person to die? For most jurors, serving on a death penalty case is one of the more difficult experiences of their lives. Language, as a vital human resource for sense-making, helps us navigate difficult experiences. It is therefore not surprising that, when facing the prospect of sending another person to his or her death, jurors rely heavily on language in order to make and then live with their decisions.

Relying on actual jurors' reflections on capital trials and my own observations of these trials, this book demonstrates how language filters, restricts, and at times is used to manipulate jurors' experiences while they serve on capital trials and again when they reflect on them afterward. When answering a call to jury duty, potential jurors enter the courtroom and immediately begin reconciling their own, often varied senses of morality with the state's command to participate in a process that could end a person's life. At the root of this process lies a conception of the law as objective and dispassionate. This ideology, which jurors learn in part from the language of attorneys and judges as well as the written instructions they are given, enables them to deny empathic and emotional connections with defendants during trail. Thus enabled, jurors use a variety of linguistic practices to distance themselves both physically and metaphysically from defendants and from their own decisions. The result is that ordinary people can perform the extraordinary act of ordering the death of another person and can then deal, for the most part, with the consequences of their decision.

I should say a little about what this book is and is not intended to do. This book is meant to provoke thought about the death penalty from an original perspective. What anthropologists do best is to identify the taken-for-granted and hold it up to critical scrutiny. By taking an in-depth look at real jurors' experiences in capital trials, this book is designed to reach beyond the legal norms that shape a U.S. death penalty trial and explore what it means in practice to send another human being to his or her death. It then considers the implications of death penalty practice for the American criminal legal system as a whole. The book is therefore strongly empirical in the sense that it is grounded firmly in observation. But it is not a statistical argument intended to support generalizations about all capital trials. Moreover, I do not intend for the book to be an explicitly persuasive project whose objective is to convince readers that the death penalty is wrong. My writing does begin, however, from the assumption that state killing, in any context, is problematic and that its justifications should be placed under critical light.

THE SIGNIFICANCE OF LANGUAGE AND DEATH PENALTY JURIES

I often get asked why, as a linguistic anthropologist, I chose to study death penalty jurors. My initial answer is an uncomplicated one, reflected in the extensive body of research on law and language.[2] Language is simply what law is made of. And as someone interested in how American legal institutions work, I was drawn to language as a natural point of entry into the topic (Drew and Heritage 1993). Moreover, individuals are made into certain kinds of persons through legal language. In a classic essay on language and law, for instance, Brenda Danet (1980) examines how words used to refer to fetuses, from "baby" to "products of conception," can create and deny life in the context of an abortion trial. Defendants in capital trials can be similarly dehumanized through language—constructed as criminals or monsters— which excludes them from categories of normal social beings (cf. Agamben 1995; Goode and Ben-Yehuda 1994; Hansen and Stepputat 2006).

When defendants are dehumanized during capital trials, their humanity is called into question well before the literal taking of their lives. They undergo a form of linguistic violence as a result of their movement through the criminal justice system. The power of this process in criminal trials more generally is enhanced when people are constructed as "criminals" before a verdict has been rendered. Consider, for example, the controversy surrounding the New York

2. For thorough reviews of this research, see Mertz and Rajah 2014 and Mertz 1994.

Police Department's handling of Dominique Strauss-Kahn before his trial had even begun. The former chief of the IMF was charged with sexually harassing a hotel employee in 2011 and was subjected to the infamous "perp walk," during which he was paraded in front of countless media personnel at the time of his arrest. The charges against him were later dropped. In a system that supposedly operates on the assumption that one is innocent until proven guilty, Strauss-Kahn (regardless of his guilt or innocence) was visibly constituted as a criminal before ever becoming a defendant (cf. Madeira 2012, 7–11).

Another straightforward answer to the question about my interest in capital jurors is that juries, though used relatively infrequently in the American legal system, are at least symbolically the "backbone" of democratic notions of justice (Barron 2003, 239; Dzur 2012). For many, the jury system stands as the embodiment of self-governance (McClanahan 2009; Vidmar and Hans 2007; 1986). It is unique among state institutions in allowing the population to have direct influence on how the state operates. For this reason, lay-judging has been implemented across the world to legitimize newly formed and developing democratic governments (Sheyn 2010; Chibundu 2008; Leib 2008). As the United State's particular form of democracy is increasingly subject to critical scrutiny, a reexamination of one of our most treasured democratic institutions seems timely.

A grimmer answer is my interest in what killing reveals about people, communities, and states. Who and how a nation kills, for instance, can tell us a lot about that nation (Otterbein 1988; Sarat and Boulanger 2005). The only Western democracy currently to employ the death penalty, the

United States legitimates this punishment in part by requiring laypeople to mete it out.[3] By calling on jurors to sentence capital defendants, the state can ensure that the act is carried out "by the people" and therefore (in theory, at least) claim democratic support for it. Where better, then, to probe the issue of state killing in the United States than from those on whom we place such a terrible burden? This burden is twofold: not only must jurors actually carry out the emotionally harrowing task of deciding on death, an incredible burden in itself (Sundby 2005), but they must also bear the weight of legitimizing state killing in a nation that is increasingly under attack, from within and outside its borders, for its fealty to it (e.g., Lanier, Bowers, and Acker 2009).

Compounding the difficulty of capital jurors' task is the meager guidance they receive from the legal system to accomplish it. Research has demonstrated that death penalty jury instructions are consistently misunderstood and that jurors consider their instructions insufficient and frustrating (Bentele and Bowers 2001; Frank and Applegate 1998; Weiner et al. 2004). The state thus thrusts laypeople (usually unwillingly) into the legal system and requires them to decide the fate of defendants according to poorly defined standards. How they accomplish this reveals a unique clash of moralities—those from jurors' everyday lives, which they may not normally reflect upon, and others that arise when jurors are asked to do something quite out of the ordinary. I am therefore not only interested in this process as support for the argument that

---

3. At the time of my research, Alabama, Florida, and Delaware were the only states that allow judges to override juries' capital sentencing verdicts. Each has since abolished judge override (Florida and Delaware in 2016, Alabama in 2017) (eji.org/reports/judge-override).

the U.S. capital punishment system is broken (though I believe it is). I also look to these moments that "shake one out of the everydayness of being moral" (Zigon 2007, 133)—when jurors must consciously reason about life and death, right and wrong (Zigon 2007, 133)—for what they can tell us about morality more generally in the contemporary United States. Studying real capital jurors provides a compelling opportunity to expose the cultural and legal assumptions about persons and punishment that guide state-sponsored killing and that permeate the criminal justice system more generally.

This book's inquiry into capital jury decision-making thus interrogates how jurors—as nonexpert laypeople—collaborate with the state in acts of violence. Anthropologists have theorized about violence as it is produced and consumed in everyday life and have shown, through ethnographic accounts of "ordinary" practices, how this production and consumption creates certain kinds of persons (Das and Kleinman 1997). This body of work tends to focus on illegitimate forms of state violence in liminal contexts, such as the violence entailed in border conflicts and the dissolution of nation-states (e.g., Besteman 1999; Das 2006; Daniel 1996). In a deviation from this perspective, I examine how people engage in an overt, legitimated practice of state violence—the death penalty—in a nation that is rarely studied as an agent of violence. Specifically, this book demonstrates how jurors, attorneys, and judges conceal and confront their involvement in the violence inherent in this practice. In rendering death verdicts, jurors are not simply pawns in the machinery of the state. They negotiate their involvement in and attitudes toward this violence in intricate, often conflicting ways.

IS CAPITAL SENTENCING A VIOLENT ACT? A POTENTIAL IRONY

The title of this section may seem absurd, as state killing is perhaps one of the more egregious forms of violence in the world. I also argued above that capital trials involve a form of linguistic violence that precedes the taking of human life. A remarkable characteristic of the death penalty in the contemporary United States however, is the obfuscation of the violence inherent to the act (Sarat 2001b). In contrast to the highly publicized executions the United States used to carry out, the death penalty is now practiced mostly at night, in small rooms enclosed within prison walls, with very few people in attendance. Excepting the few dramatized executions we might see in movies or other media (Lynch 2000), what an execution looks like is largely unknown by the general population.

Recent "botched" executions, such as Clayton Lockett's in Oklahoma, have provided further, horrifying evidence of the extent to which the workings of capital punishment are kept obscured in the United States. Lockett was executed on April 29, 2014, using an as-yet untested cocktail of drugs, which caused him to convulse and continue to speak until his death forty-three minutes after the injection. In the year leading up to his execution, the supplier of the often-used execution drug sodium thiopental ceased producing it, after which European manufacturers refused to export it to the United States for use in executions. States have since been left to scramble for experimental drugs from undisclosed suppliers. Current laws permit this secrecy; states may conceal a great deal of information about the lethal injection drugs they use, including the identity of their suppliers and the testing that the drugs have or have not undergone.[4] This legal secrecy has had ruinous consequences, as multiple recent executions have left inmates writhing and gasping for air, some dying hours after being injected.[5]

The act of execution is also shrouded within the course of capital trials. At a fundamental level, trials attenuate the violence inherent in them by turning acts of violence into bureaucratic discourse (Sarat 1995, 1107). Some kinds of violence are made overt in the courtroom. The murders for which defendants are on trial are recreated viscerally, for one. The violence of these acts is manifested in the bloody murder weapons displayed during trials, along with crime scene photos and emotional tellings from victims and witnesses. In stark contrast, however, the violence of the impending execution is conspicuously absent. I witnessed no testimony or evidence pertaining to executions in any of the trials I observed and read about. This discrepancy leads me to two related questions: When a jury sentences a defendant to death, is this itself an act of violence? More importantly, do jurors experience it as such? As I will argue in chapter 6, the specific procedures by which Texas jurors sentence capital defendants severely diminish their individual roles in the violent outcome of their decisions.

4. Paige Williams, "Witnesses to a Botched Execution," *New Yorker*, April 30, 2014.

5. Executions have similarly failed in Arizona and Ohio (Associated Press, "Three Executions Gone Wrong: Details of Lethal Injections in Arizona, Ohio, Oklahoma," July 24, 2014).

A NOTE ON RACE AND THE DEATH PENALTY

Extensive research has demonstrated that the death penalty in the United States is marred by institutionalized racial inequalities (Brewer 2004; McAdams 1998; Unnever and Cullen 2007). Cultural ideas about race, coupled with socioeconomic status, ethnic identity, and gender, affect how defendants are punished in any area of criminal law (Mustard 2001) and, as of early 2020, 70% of Texas death row inmates are people of color. It may appear, therefore, that not to talk about race explicitly in the context of the death penalty, as this book does not, is an oversight. This book, however, simply has a different goal. Instead of focusing on explicit social categories, such as race, embedded in the system of capital punishment, I aim to illuminate linguistic practices that help construct and are layered onto the racializied ideologies that pervade the system.

These linguistic practices are not themselves necessarily racialized, however. They provide a means by which jurors and others dehumanize defendants, a process that is often racialized in criminal justice contexts (Fleury-Steiner 2004). For example, chapter 5 argues that ways of referring to defendants in trial, such as "that killer," help to dehumanize defendants and thereby allow jurors to justify death sentences. Reference forms such as these, while not referring to race in and of themselves, could be used in the context of constructing a black defendant, for instance, as a dangerous monster deserving of death. It is through their use in racialized contexts, then, that these dehumanizing language forms may come to take on racist meanings.[6]

---

6. See Hill 2008 for a discussion of how covert racism is carried out through language.

My particular data, moreover, are drawn from cases in which the majority of defendants, victims, and jurors were white.[7] A systematic examination of the role of race on jurors' decisions was therefore not feasible in my research.[8] I thus hope to provide a unique perspective on state killing that can be used in dialogue with those theorizing the role of race in the dehumanization and sentencing to death of capital defendants.

ROAD MAP FOR THE BOOK

As described above, this book is about language and capital trials. The next chapter describes how I go about analyzing these phenomena. After a discussion of the death penalty in the United States and Texas as an anomalous institution within a global context, chapter 2 outlines the methods I used to study jurors' death penalty decisions. Chapter 3 discusses a contradiction inherent to death penalty jurors' task: they are asked to remain unbiased and base their decisions only on evidence, but are concurrently told that their sentencing decision is subjective and moral. Chapter 3 argues that jurors tend to eschew the second part of their contradictory instructions, believing that their purportedly subjective experiences, such as emotional reactions to witnesses and defendants, should not factor into their decisions. This contradiction is further explored in chapter 4, with a focus

---

7. None of the jurors with whom I spoke was African American. Two of them were Hispanic American and the remaining jurors were white. Of the four cases I observed, three of the defendants were white and one was African American. The victim in that case was also African American, while the other victims were white.

8. See Fleury-Steiner 2004 for an excellent treatment of this topic.

on jurors' and defendants' embodied actions during trial. Despite jurors' frequent remarks about such actions, jurors tend to think that they are not relevant to their sentencing decisions. These understandings—or misunderstandings—are related to jurors' views about the role of emotion in decision-making.

Chapters 5 and 6 discuss distancing tactics that jurors utilize to justify their sentences for death. Chapter 5 draws a parallel between physical distance and linguistic distance, demonstrating how both kinds counter the empathy with defendants that jurors might otherwise develop. These distancing practices aid in dehumanizing and ultimately calling for the execution of defendants. Chapter 6 argues that jurors also construct distance between themselves and their own decisions in order to facilitate killing another person. Grammatical constructions of agency are a critical element in this distancing process.

Chapter 7, the conclusion, returns to the question posed at the beginning of this introduction: how can one human being sentence another to death? This chapter discusses the central place that communicative practices occupy in jurors' negotiations of this seemingly impossible task. By engaging in various communicative distancing strategies, jurors deny the humanistic side of legal decision-making, which is required (though ambiguously enforced) in death penalty decisions. Thus, in the shadow of the well-shrouded act of execution, the language used in capital trials enables acts of discursive violence, in which defendants' humanity is not fully considered. These acts of discursive violence are embedded within ideologies of objectivity, impartiality, and the rule of law that are integral to the American criminal justice system. This chapter works from the assumption that jury trials—in ideology if not practice—promote certain democratic values. It provides a model that breaks apart and interrogates the linkages among culturally specific democratic ideologies, the legal system in which they are put into practice, and the forms of dehumanization intrinsic to this system.

The following conventions will also be used in transcripts throughout the book:

1. Passages in the excerpts that are of particular interest to the analysis will be in italic font.
2. Words that I was unsure about when transcribing are placed in parentheses, while empty parentheses indicate a completely indecipherable word or utterance.
3. Notes about the interactional context or words inserted by the author into the text are designated by brackets.
4. Punctuation follows conventional Standard English, with a few exceptions. Ellipses denote words that have been removed by the author. A dash indicates an abrupt stop in the talk, in which a speaker's turn or utterance is truncated.
6. An underline in the text designates that the speaker's volume is raised.

2

Doing Death in Texas: Studying Jurors in the "Death Penalty State"

THE DEATH PENALTY SCHEMA IN TEXAS

In 1972, the Supreme Court pronounced the U.S. system of capital punishment broken. The decision in *Furman v. Georgia* (408 U.S. 238 (1972)) claimed that the death penalty was implemented so arbitrarily that it violated the Eighth Amendment prohibition against cruel and unusual punishment. Capital punishment was suspended across the United States for four years until, with *Gregg v. Georgia* (428 U.S. 153 (1976)), states were permitted to reinstate the penalty as long as they supplied jurors with more specific guidelines for their sentencing decisions. The hope was that improved instructions would mitigate the haphazard nature with which death sentences had been previously administered.

At that point, states implemented bifurcated trials, which include separate culpability (or guilt/innocence) and penalty phases. In Texas, as in other states, after a jury is selected, the culpability phase of the trial is held, during which jurors decide whether to convict a defendant of a capital crime, find him guilty of a lesser offense, or acquit. This part of the trial resembles other US criminal trials in its evidentiary standards and process of deliberation.

If the defendant is convicted of capital murder, an entirely new presentation of evidence begins so that the same jurors may decide whether the defendant deserves to die. This phase can include evidence of the defendant's background, including mental illness or hardships, and the impact the murder has had on people who knew the victim. For this stage, the same jurors who decided guilt/innocence must determine the punishment. In Texas, their only two options when the defendant is found guilty of capital murder is life without the possibility of parole (LWOP)[1] or death by lethal injection. This bifurcated trial structure is illustrated in figure 2.1. Interviews I conducted with jurors that are the focus of this book concentrate primarily on jurors' sentencing decisions; however, as will become evident, the distinction between culpability and punishment phase deliberations is not always apparent to jurors themselves.

Furman and its progeny required states to adopt more rigid capital sentencing instructions to be applied in penalty phase deliberations in an effort to establish "guided discretion" for jurors in their sentencing decisions (Gregg v. Georgia (1976); see Bowers, Fleury-Steiner, and Antonio 2003;

---

1. Life without parole, or "LWOP," was implemented in Texas in 2005. Before that, defendants convicted of capital murder and who received life sentences would be eligible for parole after an extended prison term. I spoke to some jurors who served on capital trials before the implementation of LWOP, and many of them disclosed that they would not have given their defendant death if LWOP had been an option.

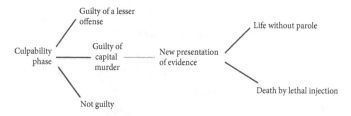

FIGURE 2.1 Bifurcated trial structure

Luginbuhl and Howe 1995; Lynch and Haney 2000; Weiner et al. 2004). Whereas most states responded by implementing a weighing system, according to which jurors weigh aggravating versus mitigating circumstances, Texas adopted the "special issue" framework. At the time I carried out my fieldwork in 2008–2010, this schema required jurors in sentencing phase deliberations to answer two special issue questions[2] that led them to a sentence of LWOP or death.[3] The first of these is commonly referred to as the "future danger" question, which reads as follows:

> Do you find from the evidence beyond a reasonable doubt that there is a probability that the defendant would commit criminal acts of violence that would constitute a continuing threat to society?

If jurors answer yes to this question, they go on to the second, or "mitigation" question, which asks:

> Do you find from the evidence, taking into consideration all of the evidence, including the circumstances of the offense, the

2. Tex. Crim. Proc. Code Ann. Art 37. 071 (2)(b)(1).
3. These questions have been amended by the legislature since their inception in 1976; the cases I observed in 2008–2010 utilized the instructions as they currently stand.

defendant's character and background, and the personal moral culpability of the defendant, that there is a sufficient mitigating circumstance or circumstances to warrant that a sentence of life imprisonment rather than a death sentence be imposed?

If the jurors unanimously answer yes to question one and no to question two,[4] the defendant receives a death sentence. If the jurors answer these questions in any other way, the defendant is sentenced to life without parole. Texas jurors are thus never explicitly asked whether they will put the defendant to death; the death sentence is mediated by these special issue questions.

In addition to its bifurcated structure and specialized jury instructions, a capital trial in Texas differs considerably from other criminal trials in regards to one other component: its voir dire. Though not all are carried out in identical fashion, those I witnessed and read about in transcripts followed the same overall structure. In a capital voir dire, potential jurors are summoned (by mail) as a group (usually about two hundred at a time) to the courthouse at a designated time. At this point, the judge and both sides' attorneys address the entire panel in turn. Each usually explains the capital trial process superficially, including issues such as lesser offenses and minimum sentences. Jurors are also polled as a group at this point about their categorical opposition to the death penalty and any conflicts they may have with serving. Some jurors are dismissed at this time, either because they say they categorically do not believe in the

4. If jurors cannot come to a unanimous decision on either of these questions, the defendant receives a life sentence. The Texas statute, however, prohibits attorneys and judges from informing jurors of this fact. Therefore, many jurors feel pressure to reach unanimity because they fear a mistrial if they do not do so. This is an incredibly contentious issue for attorneys, one that deserves its own analysis, but it does not fit within the scope of this book.

death penalty or because they have significant conflicts with the trial schedule.

Not surprisingly, perhaps, during a trial I observed in a relatively liberal college city, a much greater majority of the jury panel was excused at this point for their opposition to the death penalty than in any other trial I observed. Even though the initial jury pool included more people with anti-death penalty beliefs, the resultant group from which the jurors were chosen more closely resembled the other counties I visited, with fairly healthy support for the death penalty. Although further discussion of this issue is not within the scope of this book, this initial "death qualifying" process starts the jury pool out as an already narrowed group, one that for many critics denies the defendant their Sixth Amendment right to a jury that represents a cross-section of the community (e.g., Salgado 2005).

After the panel questioning, jurors are given extensive questionnaires (sometimes twenty to thirty pages) that they fill out and return to the court, which supplies each team of attorneys with copies. With these questionnaires, the attorneys prepare for perhaps the most extensive phase of the trial, the individual juror questioning (I indeed encountered capital voir dires that lasted longer than the presentations of evidence). In this stage, each venire person is brought into the courtroom individually and questioned extensively, for about an hour, about his or her questionnaire, the types of evidence jurors may hear about during the trial, and the person's feelings about the death penalty. It is during this stage that the jury is assembled, each side's attorneys having a number of peremptory challenges they can use to strike jurors they do not want. The death qualification process continues during this extensive individual questioning, the implications of which will be discussed in later chapters (cf. Sandys and McClelland 2003).

STATE KILLING IN THE UNITED STATES AND TEXAS

As discussed in the introduction, the system and implementation of the death penalty in the United States remains to a large degree hidden from the population. Indeed, Sarat (2001b, 191) argues that the "survival of capital punishment in the United States depends, in part, on its relative invisibility." Despite continued (though decreasing) numbers of executions in the United States—in 2019, the nation performed the sixth highest number of executions worldwide[5]—the population's attitude remains predominantly indifferent to it (Dow and Dow 2002). This is due in part to the opacity of this state practice. Little is understood, both academically and in popular culture, about how the death penalty actually operates (Gross and Ellsworth 1994), save occasional reports of botched executions and exonerated defendants and dramatized executions in movies and television shows. The numerous and lengthy steps between charging a defendant with a capital crime and actually executing him[6] remain for the most part obscured.[7]

The death house in Texas—where the state's executions are carried out—is located in Huntsville in "Walls" unit, the

5. The United States executed twenty-two people in 2019, ranking it sixth behind China (whose total is not disclosed), Iran, Saudi Arabia, Iraq, and Egypt (Amnesty International, 2020).

6. Though there are occasionally women capital defendants in Texas (there were 6 women (of 214 total) on death row in Texas as of March 2020), the majority are men, and all of those I dealt with during my fieldwork were men. I will therefore use the male pronoun to refer to capital defendants throughout the book.

7. A notable exception is the extensive survey work the Capital Jury Project has completed, which has questioned postverdict jurors from numerous states. For an overview of the project, see Bowers 1995, and for a list of the project's publications, see its website at http://www.albany.edu/scj/13194.php.

oldest of Texas's prisons. Huntsville itself is home to the Texas Department of Criminal Justice, which employs a majority of its population. At the time of an execution— 6:00 p.m., always during rush hour—the town shows virtually no indication of what is taking place. Other than a few protesters scattered across the street from Walls in the area the prison has designated for them, the execution leaves no trace beyond the cement barriers of the death house. Traffic passes steadily by, drivers seemingly occupied with end-of-the-day concerns; the electricity no longer flickers, as it was rumored once to do; there is no signal of the end of a life. Despite jurors' inside perspective on part of the death penalty process, they too are shielded from the act of execution itself.

The United States is currently the only industrialized nation in the West to retain capital punishment. Within the United States, though twenty-eight states retain capital punishment on the books, the majority of executions are carried out in very few states, all located in the southern part of the country. Texas, specifically, has held a unique position as the killingest state in the United States since 1976, the year that ended the nationwide moratorium. The following section investigates Texas as an anomaly in the current American death penalty landscape. While Texas is special in regards to the death penalty, the issues raised in this book are not necessarily contained to Texas. They in fact shed light on endemic, often unarticulated assumptions and values that undergird the US criminal justice system more generally. Thus while keeping an analytic eye on the regionally and culturally specific elements of capital punishment in Texas, an aim of this book is also to identify those practices and ideologies that may cross regional and cultural lines.

ANOMALIES WITHIN ANOMALIES

To explore the sociocultural topography of Texas capital punishment, I begin with an anomaly within an anomaly: a life verdict in a Texas capital case. This rare phenomenon is in fact anomalous on a number of levels. First is the persistence of capital punishment in the United States amid a community of nations that increasingly considers the death penalty a violation of universal human rights. As the only Western democracy to continue the use of capital punishment, the United States is in the company of China, the Democratic Republic of Congo, Iran, Iraq, and Saudi Arabia, some of the worst human rights violators in the world. The United States remains exceptional even in its frequent use of life without parole as a felony sentence, as many nations have deemed this sentence a human rights violation as well (Steiker and Steiker 2013). Explanations for US exceptionalism in regard to human rights and the death penalty are increasingly debated (e.g., Ignatieff 2005); some include the elevated homicide rate in the United States in relation to other Western nations, the symbolic value of the death penalty in a nation in which crime is a key political issue (Sarat 2001a, 2001b), and individual states' criminal lawmaking autonomy within our federal system (Steiker 2005).

The federalism theory of American exceptionalism leads us to the second level of anomaly: Texas's disproportionate use and support of capital punishment in comparison to other US states. Texas's distinction in this regard certainly exists in perception, but the extent to which Texas is truly the picture of a death penalty anomaly deserves a closer look. Historically, Texas jurors have tended to give defendants death more times than not when the sentence is available.

From 2005 (when LWOP was implemented in Texas) to 2016, Texas jurors sentenced capital defendants to death 80 percent of the time.[8] However, death sentencing rates have dropped dramatically since their peak in 1999, with 4 death sentences and 4 LWOP sentences given in 2019 (tcadp.org).

The picture of Texas as the "epicenter of capital punishment," dubbed as such in a recent *Atlantic* article (Cohen 2014), is not without complexity and contradictions. Texas is a standout in numbers of executions since the countrywide abolition and reinstatement of the death penalty in the 1970s—its 569 executions more than quadruple those of the next killingest state, Virginia. However, when comparing the number of death *sentences* given to capital defendants in the last decade, California and Florida are leaders;[8a] these states also house the most death row inmates in the nation. Texas's number of death sentences has reduced significantly in the last 20 years—from forty-eight in 1999 to four in 2019.[9] While California and Florida historically show significant use of the death penalty as a sentence for capital crimes, Texas far and away exceeds all other states in number of actual executions. The rate of executions in the United States has been in dramatic decline in the past 20 years, but Texas's numbers have not consistently followed this decline. In 1999, Texas executions accounted for 36 percent of the national total. In 2013, the countrywide number reduced by over half and Texas executed nearly 50 percent of this new low. These data support the belief, expressed to me by countless Texans during my fieldwork, that while other states, such as California, support the death penalty, it is Texas that truly gets it done.

8. Texasdefender.org.
8a. Governor Newsome of California issued an executive order halting the death penalty in 2019.
9. ibid.

Unquestionably intact is the *idea* of Texas as the kill-ingest state among insiders and outsiders alike. Proud Texans brag about its status compared to the rest of the country, especially its expeditiousness in carrying out executions, while those Texas natives who distance themselves from this identity still sustain it in their resistance to it. Though most jurors I spoke with had more nuanced positions on the death penalty, the "just fry 'em" attitude about capital offenders often attributed to Texas is not baseless. One juror, Bob (I will use pseudonyms for all defendants, jurors, and attorneys represented in the book), confessed to me that he was approached outside the courtroom while on a break during the trial by a man he did not know with no apparent connection to the case. From his attire, it seemed that the man was either a current or former government employee. Bob explained:

> I mean, I usually go outside either to check my phone or just to get out for a minute 'cause I don't like being inside that much, but this old boy walks by, and, I think he works for the county here, he says, you know, and he's wearing his old uniform from when he worked at TDC [Texas Department of Corrections], just 'cause it's good work clothes I guess, but he says, *I don't know why y'all are even up here. They oughta kill every one of ('em).* Said geez, and he said I'll tell you what (I'm from right down there) blah blah blah, and I'm just looking at him like, you don't even know who I am. You're just, you know, regurgitating all this stuff here and [laughs].

This trial was held in a very small, one-stoplight town. Most inhabitants would have been well aware of its occurrence and the details of the crime. This man, however, did not limit his comments to the defendant in this particular case, but expressed a not too uncommon belief that all capital defendants should be executed.

And while rare, this attitude did surface in some of my interviews. I spoke with one juror who had served on a case years before that sentenced its defendant to death. He described the start of their penalty phase deliberations:

> The minute we walked in the jury room one man said, *Let's kill him*. Before anybody discussed anything. And, myself, didn't think that was right? And nobody said nothing.

Though I cannot know for certain whether this actually happened as described, this was not the only account I was given of such immediate, resolute desire for a death sentence within a jury.

While this unabashed fervor for the death penalty indeed exists in Texas and finds its way onto juries, simply labeling Texas a killer among nonkilling states does little to further a discussion about capital punishment in the United States. Questions that deserve to be addressed include what does focusing on the symbolic weight of Texas as a killing machine take away from the overall picture of capital punishment in the United States? Why are we so attached to branding Texas a killer when, for instance, California jurors have shown just as much, if not more commitment to the death penalty, at least at the trial level?

A third level of anomaly concerns jurors giving life sentences in Texas capital cases. As stated previously, Texas juries overwhelmingly give capital defendants death over life—80 percent of the time between 2005 and 2015. Among the life cases I was made aware of during my research, jurors in support of life were exceptional within juries themselves; life sentences were rendered most commonly when one to three jurors voted for life against a death-supporting majority. Death sentences in Texas require a unanimous jury vote, so even one holdout for life can secure an LWOP sentence. Juror behavior was reinforced by the attitudes of many Texans, from which of course the jury pools are drawn. Similar to Bob's experience described above, Nancy—a juror who served on the case I will review below—encountered outsiders to the case who subscribed to an "execute all of them" belief in the death penalty. She reported that after her trial, people were shocked at the life verdict her jury rendered: "I had a lot of people say, how in the world?" she remarked. "The guy confesses to five murders" and he gets life. This is not to say Texas jurors easily and unproblematically give death sentences to defendants. Most jurors commented during their interviews that weighing a capital sentencing decision was one of the more difficult experiences of their lives. This makes the issue all that more perplexing. If giving a death sentence is extremely difficult, how does it happen 80 percent of the time?

ONE TEXAS LIFE CASE

I look now to one Texas life case for what this apparent anomaly can tell us about the sociolegal world(s) in which a life sentence is rendered. Only weeks after I arrived in Texas, I sat in on a capital case—what I will call the Lewis case—midway through its sentencing phase presentation of evidence. Out of the four trials I followed closely during my fieldwork, this case was the only one that resulted in a life sentence. The trial was held in a fairly well-populated, urban west Texas county, but had been transferred from the county of indictment, which was located farther north in a slightly less populated area. The defendant was a white male in his upper twenties, not a Texas resident. After killing two people in another state, a crime to which he pled guilty and was given a life sentence, he was being tried in Texas for murdering multiple members of a family in their home. He had a calm, almost soft demeanor during trial and had remarkable artistic abilities. He spent most of his time in the courtroom sketching, and some of his drawings were presented as mitigating evidence, showcasing his talent and thus potential worth to others.

During their punishment deliberations, the jury answered yes to the first special issue question, deeming Lewis a "future danger" to society. They did not agree on the mitigation question, however, thus ending upon a sentence of LWOP. I interacted closely with some of the defense attorneys on the case and a consultant from a nearby university working with the defense. Only two jurors from the case agreed to be interviewed by me, both of whom supported a death sentence for the defendant: Nancy, the juror we heard from above, who was sympathetic to those who voted for life, and Maria, who treated the LWOP verdict with disbelief and exasperation. The foreman—the only man on the jury—spoke openly to the press after the verdict about his frustration with the LWOP sentence. He asserted to a local paper that a single juror kept the jury from voting for a death sentence, which was what the "majority" of jurors wanted.[10] Multiple media outlets subsequently reported that the defendant's life was saved by a "lone juror." The foreman's story was contested by both of the jurors with whom I spoke, however.

10. Logan G. Carver, "Single Vote Spares Killer's Life," *Lubbock Avalanche-Journal*, October 8, 2009.

They stated that *three* jurors supported an LWOP sentence, one of whom was indeed particularly vocal and recalcitrant. In attempting to understand this anomalous phenomenon—a life verdict in a Texas capital case—I found that two kinds of exceptionalism are potentially necessary for jurors to render a life sentence in Texas. There has to be at least one exceptional *juror* among the twelve, and the *defendant* must also be considered an exception. What it does not seem to take is an exceptionally mundane or tidy crime—this was one of the more grisly crimes I encountered in my field-work, and yet the defendant received a life sentence.

First, in regards to the exceptional juror: in the Lewis case, as mentioned above, at least one and potentially more jurors voiced early in the deliberations that they were going to vote for a life sentence and that, to quote Nancy, "we were never going to change their mind." As numerous defense attorneys told me, it was important to instill in jurors that their individual vote is theirs and theirs alone. This is not an easy message to convey, however. This is the one case I en-countered in which a juror who supported life did not change her vote over the course of deliberations and thus held the jury against a death sentence. The jurors from the Lewis case related that the particularly obstinate juror began deliberations with the stance that she would not give death—because of her beliefs, according to Maria, and her acceptance of the powerful mitigating evidence, according to Nancy. Both revealed this holdout juror's assertion that nobody was going to change her mind. I saw attorneys at-tempt to coach potential life jurors into this kind of stance, but none were able to maintain their votes against antago-nistic majorities. A life sentence may thus necessitate a juror who can both withstand the death qualification process and then support a life sentence against potentially combative fellow jurors.

And in regards to the exceptional defendant: Lewis was described by Nancy as someone who "doesn't look like a murderer," "like a pretty normal ol' guy." Maria likewise said he "seemed like a nice guy just by the, by the way he looked"; "he might be a nice okay person. Have problems, but who doesn't have problems." After the presentation of the mitigation evidence in the sentencing portion of the trial, Nancy viewed him as "a victim himself." She further explained that her view of the defendant was altered as the prosecution and defense each presented their evidence.

In order to obtain a life verdict in a capital trial, the jury has to think of the defendant as an exceptional result of an exceptional constellation of experiences (cf. Conley Riner and Vartkessian 2018). Many people have bad childhoods, jurors consistently declared. Many have had drug problems; many are poor and come from broken families. But those others with similarly rough lives, the logic holds, do not murder multiple people. As Nancy conveyed, even though the defendant in her case had a particularly difficult life, "At some point, you're still responsible [banging on the table], even if you had a lousy life. At some point you still have to make good decisions."

To combat this pervasive logic, mitigation experts who organize the presentation of mitigating evidence attempt to weave a diverse complex of information into a narrative, not of causation, but of explanation. We all live within a network of events, people, and experiences that inform our choices and actions as our lives progress. Defense teams must argue for the exceptionalism of their defendants; they must place a defendant at the center of a network of experiences singular to his life—different even from his other family members, and different enough to explain the criminal behavior in which he engaged. Nancy spoke of this fine line a defense team must walk in order to convince jurors of a life sentence: "Where, where do you draw the line between accountability for your actions and, you know, you, you don't stand a chance of making good decisions based on all this stuff?" Nancy further commented on the Lewis defense team's successful strategy in presenting such exceptionalism: "The defense did a real good job of saying all these people were raised in the same house. But he was the scapegoat. He was the one the dad didn't like. He was the one that dad took everything out on."

At the same time however, what makes designing a mitigation case so tricky is that the defendant must also be seen as similar enough to others that he retains the empathic and remorseful emotions that jurors seek out of most capital defendants.[11] Nancy, who again supported a death sentence, described the defendant as follows: it's "not that he didn't have a conscience, but it was just almost like emotionally he was just dead." She further described his abnormal behavior in the courtroom:

> A normal person wouldn't have done what he did, and, and, and you see this guy that is kind of nonemotional either direction, and you see him as kind of as not as a normal person then. Not that he's crazy, but that it's just like, he could, he was just totally separated from, from what you'd think normal emotions would be in seeing all that and reliving it.

I heard this refrain repeatedly from jurors who served on other cases—all of whose defendants received death sentences.

11. Chapters 3 and 4 will discuss emotion and empathy in depth.

It seems a jury must thus also view a defendant as exhibiting "normal" emotional responses within and outside the trial in order for them to consider a life sentence.

The particular perspectives it takes to render a life sentence in a Texas capital trial reveal the underlying logics by which death sentences are so frequently given. Perhaps, as Richland suggests about anomalous cases more generally, a greater frequency and visibility of life sentences might "alter how the norms come to be understood"[11a] (Burns et al. 2008, 315), for example, the symbolic position of Texas as an outlier within the landscape of capital punishment in the United States. There exists perhaps a causal loop of symbology and practice in Texas—Texas is different because we think it is different, and because we think it is different, we explain practices in Texas as anomalous.

THE DEATH PENALTY AND IDENTITY IN TEXAS

As discussed above, Texas's state identity comprises in part its dedication to the swift, efficient implementation of capital punishment. This section briefly explores the degree to which jurors' individual identities are informed by their engagement in this process. Becoming a juror involves in large part an occupation of a variety of identities, some real, some imagined or symbolic, some local to a town or county or state, some national and American. These identities have different reference points, all of which are linked in some way to place. As I sat through trials and talked to jurors in Texas while conducting my fieldwork, I thought about what it meant for these people to be involved in death penalty trials.

[11a.] Current trends in sentencing rates indeed beg this question.

How do they identify themselves within this process? How do their identities change or merge or shift upon participating in this institutional ordeal?

In sifting through these questions, especially in trying to maintain my own identity as an anthropologist while asking them, I realized that it is impossible to omit place from the equation. It seeps into how jurors talk about their experiences; it's in the casual and often jocular conversations the judges and attorneys have when court is out of session, either in the courtroom or in chambers. I was saturated in it as I drove through the vast Texas landscapes from county to county; I was in it on the bucolic ranch roads that took me to a juror's house two miles in from the main road, then equally so when I impatiently stood in the line that wraps around the Austin criminal courthouse in order to be fed through the metal detector. Texas jurors often constituted themselves in terms of a place-identity, that is, as inhabitants of the state of Texas. Abstract identities and cultural notions such as moral beings, justice, and criminality are often invoked through references to place. It is as if these ideals must occupy or inhabit some place, real or imaginary, in order to make sense and to become recognizable referents for a shared identity (cf. Fox 2004).

I thus find it helpful to speak of *occupying* identities, especially when so-called laypeople become entangled in some institutional process. Carr (2009) speaks of a similar process when former drug addicts become institutional social workers within rehab programs, and as such must find discursive ways to "inhabit," as she writes, this institutional identity. As soon as the jury selection process starts, different kinds of people are required to occupy the institutional identity of being a juror, and there is some shared sense of how this occupation is carried out. This process starts far before the jurors' summons are sent; what a juror is, and what a juror is in Texas, exist in the minds of these people well before they come into the courthouse to sit through questioning. Prior to walking through the courtroom doors, jurors have acquired notions of what it means to be inside the jury box from a variety of sources, such as their families and the media.

Jurors are locals in the most literal sense, in that they are drawn from a pool of county inhabitants and must have resided in that county for at least thirty days in order to serve. However, the ideal jury, as attorneys often point out during jury selections, comes from a "cross-section" of the community; therefore it should not be homogeneous, as a more classic sense of locality might suggest. This cross-section, however, is itself an ideal construction, since in death penalty trials especially, certain components of these cross-sections are automatically excused. Jurors are weeded out that have extreme views about the death penalty,[12] or cannot afford to miss work, or have children at home, for instance. After these automatic excusals, lawyers then tend to strike certain categories of people using their peremptories, such as women, African Americans, teachers, lawyers, police officers, ultraconservatives, and so on.[13] Even though this ideal of a cross-section of

12. Though the law requires that jurors who have extreme views about the death penalty either way—that they would always give it or always give life—be excused, many argue that juries are stacked toward death because it is much easier to convince venire persons who are death supporters that they could consider life in some hypothetical case than convince those who do not believe in the death penalty to give death.

13. Though the *Batson* Supreme Court decision (*Batson v. Kentucky*, 476 U.S. 79 (1986)) should technically keep attorneys from categorically striking jurors according to their social identities, such as race or gender, I never once saw a *Batson* challenge succeed in practice.

the community may not be satisfyingly reached, juries do retain some level of diversity. As one juror from an exceptionally small Texas county noted when asked how the jury defined reasonable doubt:

For us it was what's reasonable to our group there. Because we were pretty diverse. I mean sure, we're all country people. We all live here, but there's a lot of different backgrounds and a lot of different educational levels, a lot of different work experience. Life experience. And while perhaps we are in general more conservative than people in Berkeley, I don't know that, you know, we're that hhhfar differenthhh.

This brief interview excerpt exhibits how different levels of place can be invoked to make sense of an experience and project a certain identity. First, the juror references "our group there," identifying the jury as a body through a deictic reference to the courthouse or jury room "there." "There" serves to locate the jury in a specific place and point in time, that is, the jury room during the trial. In addition, the inclusive pronoun "our" both serves to create unity among the group of jurors and to distinguish this group from others who do not belong. Next, the juror describes the difference and similarity among the jurors, first through the term "country people," which is an identifying referent to a general category of people that relies on both a physical and imagined place called "the country"; this notion of country people includes what Fox (2004, 28) has identified as "prototypical independent and free Americans." "We all live here," the juror goes on, referencing the country in general as well as the specific location of Horrace County. While recognizing some potential similarities among the jurors based on their being from the same place, the juror rejects the thought that this means they are not diverse in any way. "There's a lot of different backgrounds," he says, which includes different educational levels, work experience, and life experience. Through the use of the pronoun "we," the juror further identifies the jury members as a collective and continues to define points of commonality among them, which next includes the fact that they are conservative. He does this through the practice of differentiation introduced above, defining similarity by invoking some distinct other. This other, not surprisingly, is defined through a place name, Berkeley. "Perhaps we are in general more conservative than people in Berkeley," he says, which echoes an often used comparison in Texas, that is, that we are *not* California. Berkeley as a cultural reference also serves here to set up a polarity of extremes, Berkeley being an archetypical symbol of liberalism, which positions Texas as the archetype of conservatism. But, he continues, "I don't know that, you know, we're that far different." In other words, Texans aren't entirely different from others throughout the nation, even those in Berkeley.

But Texas's customary image as a loner under constant threat from outsiders remains an undercurrent to discussions about Texas capital punishment. It has often been used to explain the state's exceptional use of the death penalty and its archetypically "tough" approach to crime (Sween 2014). Following George W. Bush, Governor Rick Perry became Texas's mascot for swift and severe justice. In a televised debate to support his bid for the republican presidential nomination in 2012, Governor Perry was asked whether having overseen more than two hundred executions during his tenure made it hard for him to sleep at night. When the questioner read out this statistic, the audience erupted into cheers. After responding that he experienced no unease due to his lengthy execution record, he went on to describe criminal justice in Texas:

> But in the state of Texas, if you come into *our* state, and you kill one of *our* children, you kill a police officer, you're involved with another crime and you kill one of *our* citizens, you will face the ultimate justice in the state of Texas. And that is you will be executed. [Loud cheers]

In this public address, Perry created a unified collective that is Texas through the use of the inclusive pronoun "our." Significantly, he addressed a hypothetical criminal in the second person, "you," thus excluding him (I would assume his hypothetical criminal is a man) as a member of this collective. The criminal is thus seen as an outsider who enters the state in order to cause harm to its citizens. His mobilization of Texas as a unified place with unified goals for hard justice was met with an exuberant round of cheers. Thus even though the number of death sentences actually handed out in Texas and in the country as a whole has decreased over the past few years, support for the death penalty, as evidenced through the response to Perry's answer, still exists as an ideology that unites Texans according to their underlying values of swift and strict justice.

RESEARCH DESIGN AND METHODS

The data presented in this book were collected as part of my dissertation research, which involved twelve months of fieldwork from 2009 to 2010 in and around Houston, Texas.[14] I

---

14. This research was generously supported by the Wenner Gren Foundation and the National Institute of Justice.

chose Houston as my base because, at the time, it was one of two hubs for death penalty litigation and policymaking in Texas, Austin being the other.[15] I obtained contacts with attorneys during my pilot research in 2008, which involved a legal internship with the Texas Defender Service, a nonprofit organization in Houston that provides trial and appeal aid to capital defenders.[16] Texas Defender Service attorneys were crucial in providing me with information, trial documents, and research assistance as my fieldwork progressed.

During these twelve months, I attended four capital trials from start to finish and conducted postverdict interviews with jurors. This work took me to six different Texas counties in central, east, and west Texas, thereby introducing me to a wide variety of areas of the state. I did not, however, have much exposure to the areas of Texas along the Mexican border, about which a preponderance of the anthropological work on Texas has been written (e.g., Martinez 2009; Spener 2009; Saldívar 1997; Paredes 1995).

The research and analysis relied on a variety of ethnographic and linguistic anthropological methods, including participant observation in death penalty trials, interviews of jurors and other trial participants, and qualitative linguistic analyses of transcribed interviews and courtroom interaction (see Sidnell 2010; Bernard 2006; Duranti 1997). This integration of methods serves, in the absence of access to actual capital jury rooms,[17] to provide the clearest window into jurors' decision-making processes.

---

15. Texas has since seen the expansion of the office of Regional Public Defense for Capital Cases, which provides defense for indigents charged with capital crimes (rpdo.org).

16. Texasdefender.org.

17. See 18 U.S.C. 1508 (2000) for a federal statute barring videotaping of jury deliberations.

PARTICIPANT OBSERVATION

The primary method of both cultural and linguistic anthropologists is participant observation, the goal of which is to immerse oneself in a cultural context while still maintaining a degree of analytic distance. When engaged in this method, the ethnographer establishes an identity within the cultural context that straddles (not easily) the dividing line between insider and outsider positions (e.g., Geertz 1973; DeWalt and DeWalt 2002; Agar 1980). For this project, I conducted participant observation in four capital trials, in which I was engaged from the start of jury selection to the reading of the sentencing verdicts; I audio-recorded one of the trials and obtained official transcripts of the others.[18] Three of these resulted in death sentences, one in a life sentence. One was located in a very sparsely populated, fairly rural central-Texas town, another in the capital city, a third in a good-sized college town in western Texas, and the last in another college town of comparable size in the central part of the state.[19] I worked very closely with the defense attorneys on these trials, attending strategy meetings, assisting with jury selection, providing assistance to defendants' family members, meeting with witnesses, and aiding in drafting legal documents, including jury instructions. These experiences provided me with a substantial background against which to interpret jurors' remarks and analyses of trial language.

18. The only trial I could not obtain a transcript of was the one in which the defendant received a life sentence, as court transcripts are not produced for cases that do not go up for appeal.

19. Though trial information and transcripts are part of the public record, I will keep details about the trials as ambiguous as possible in order to discourage any linkage between the data I present and the identities of the jurors I interviewed.

Participating in these trials was an intensely emotional experience for everyone involved, including myself.[20] My emotional reactions often led me to have conflicting feelings about my level of involvement (or lack thereof) in these trials, as well as about my alliance with the defense teams. I was certainly not modeling early anthropology's participant-observer, who attempts complete impartiality and supposedly suppresses all bias in her analysis (Malinowski 1935). I was, instead, aligning with postcolonial, postmodern versions of the ethnographer, who must accept her positioning in the field and fit it somehow into her meaning-making process (e.g., Rabinow 1977). The perspectives presented in this book are drawn primarily from jurors' narratives of their experiences, and the analyses are designed to explicate the capital trial process from jurors' vantage points. But my own, necessarily situated, experiences nonetheless bleed into my interpretations of the issues presented here. While I interacted extensively with prosecutors throughout my fieldwork, for instance, I was much more intimately involved with each case from the defense side. So, while I anchor each of my analyses in jurors' depictions of their experiences, I make use of my own experiences with the Texas criminal justice system as an interpretive backdrop, which is disproportionately the product of my interactions with the defense teams.

20. For example, at the conclusion of the punishment phase of the first trial I attended, I was invited to sit with the attorneys while they impatiently and restlessly waited for the jurors' verdict. I felt out of place and was unsure of what to do, so I offered my computer's music library to the lead counsel, who was pacing, not knowing what to do with himself either. He sat, headphones in his ears, sifting through my "eclectic" list of songs, as he called it, sometimes singing along. I'm not exactly sure if it helped him through the process, though it seemed to in some way.

Balancing my situated placement within the world of Texas capital punishment with a scholarly approach to the topic was not merely an abstract, cerebral effort. It had implications for my practices in the field. How was I to act, for instance, when I encountered the victim's mother in the bathroom, knowing she had been eyeing me sitting with the defense for the entirety of the trial? And how was I to behave with the defendants, for whom I developed a fair amount of sympathy during the trials, while trying to maintain a professional and personal level of distance? A scene from my field notes conveys an element of this phenomenological trouble I experienced during fieldwork:

> I handed a defendant a piece of chocolate, joking to him about how much he had been eating. Meanwhile, at the witness stand, a psychologist testified to the judge about how scientific research that had for decades convinced jurors that defendants would commit future acts of violence was grossly unreliable and decisions that had utilized it should be considered unconstitutional. At that moment, I was attending both to my relationship with the defendant, which mostly consisted of keeping him calm during the course of the trial, and my analytic observance of the testimony going on.

I constantly tacked back and forth between differing stances toward my experience, often deciding that one was for some reason or another more appropriate in a given situation. As will be seen through the interviews presented in this book, jurors were often similarly phenomenologically challenged, having to monitor their own thinking and judgments, convincing themselves that a particular "objective stance," for instance, was needed, while a more empathic one should be suppressed.

In addition to engaging in trials, I immersed myself in the Texas system of crime and punishment more generally. I spoke with a variety of attorneys and judges in informal settings, such as bars or meetings not related to trials. I stood and talked with protestors during two executions outside Walls. I also visited the death house inside Walls, viewing the cell in which inmates are kept until their scheduled execution time and the death chamber with its cross-shaped gurney. I toured the rest of the unit and visited two other prisons in Texas that house death row inmates.[21] Last, the majority of my personal engagements throughout my time in Texas were with capital attorneys. I forged some lasting friendships as they expressed their tribulations working within a system they viewed as deeply flawed.

INTERVIEWS

In addition to the "deep hanging out" (Wogan 2004) that filled my days in Texas, I conducted interviews with jurors, attorneys, judges, and prison staff. All interviews were audio-recorded, in order to obtain verbatim renderings of what each interviewee said. My primary interview data consisted of postverdict interviews with jurors who served on the four cases in which I participated, as well as jurors from additional cases.[22] In total, I interviewed twenty-one jurors from nine death penalty cases. These interviews often occurred only

---

21. Texas's death row is currently maintained at the Polunsky unit in Livingston. The psychiatric facility, Jester IV, in Richmond, houses death row inmates who require mental health treatment.

22. Jurors' names were obtained from public records, and I located their contact information using Internet search tools.

days or weeks after the trials had concluded. I was thus able to reduce participants' memory limitations, though all retrospective interviews must be analyzed with an eye to this potential problematic factor (Haney, Sontag, and Costanzo 1994). In the first stage of these interviews, I asked open-ended questions about the jurors' general experiences serving on capital trials. This stage was developed in order to discern what parts of the trial experience were most salient to the juror him- or herself, rather than imposing researcher-based categories onto the jurors' responses. This model of interviewing is based on the paradigm of person-centered ethnography, which investigates what features of a sociocultural context are salient to its inhabitants (Hollan 2001, 48; LeVine 1982). This approach attempts to "avoid unnecessary reliance on overly abstract . . . constructs" created by the researcher (Hollan 2001, 49). The goal of this stage of interviews was to have the jurors "construct their responses in their own ways" (Fleury-Steiner 2002, 555) in order to ascertain what was significant to jurors' decision-making from both within and external to the trial. The second stage of the interviews focused on the jurors' understanding of the language of their jury instructions.[23] These questions were designed to interrogate how jurors processed and interpreted their instructions and what impact this had on their decision-making processes.

In addition to speaking with jurors, I interviewed judges and lawyers involved in a variety of death penalty trials, including those on which the jurors I interviewed served. I additionally interviewed people involved in varied aspects of the system of capital punishment, such as prison wardens

---

23. Jury instructions are also often called "charges." I will use these terms interchangeably throughout the book.

and guards. These interviews were conducted in order to obtain contextual information regarding jurors' knowledge about and interpretation of various aspects of the death penalty process. These interviews were less structured than the jurors' interviews, the main purpose being to elicit interviewees' impressions of defendants, their trials, and the implementation of the death penalty.

Transcripts of the audio-recorded interviews were analyzed with an eye to both linguistic and content-based aspects of the data. Instead of coding each interview according to subjects that I, the analyst, found important, I looked to the actual wording of interviewees' responses to deem what was important to them (Briggs 1986). By comparatively analyzing language used in the trials and juror interviews, I gained an understanding of what specific linguistic forms and techniques were used in trials to construct defendants as particular kinds of (non)persons and which of these linguistic practices jurors found significant to their decisions. This analysis additionally illuminated what extralegal factors (such as jurors' own ideas about criminality and morality) contributed to jurors' decisions. The analysis also explored the extent to which jurors (mis)understood their instructions, what specific parts of the trial affected these (mis)understandings, and how these (mis)understandings informed their jurors' decisions.

While in many fields interview responses are taken at face value, assumed unproblematically to represent sociocultural and linguistic truths of a given community, linguistic anthropologists treat interviews as speech events in their own right, with their own contextual limitations (Briggs 1986). The interview data in this book are therefore offered as representing each juror's *ideologies* about capital trials, recognizing that these ideologies may be constructed in part due to the interview situation itself, with me (as a female researcher from California, etc.) as a piece of its contextual configuration (cf. Duranti 1997, 102–110).

After talking at length with many jurors, my most surprising and revelatory finding, which will be examined in the remaining chapters of the book, was that jurors struggle, often emotionally, with the conflict between literally facing defendants during trial and then having to distort, diminish, or negate these interactions in order to sentence those same defendants to death. One juror's admission—that the conjunctive acts of literally facing a man and then sending him to death were the most difficult of his life—exemplifies this conflict: "That's the hardest thing I've ever had to do, to look at a man and, you know, know that I'm saying, you know, I don't think you should live." My research revealed that language plays a significant role in negotiating these moral conflicts and thus in facilitating death sentences.

TRANSCRIPT CONVENTIONS

Throughout the book, transcript excerpts from trials and juror interviews will be presented, using the following speaker abbreviations:

P (prosecutor)
D (defense attorney)
J (Juror)
C (Court (Judge))
R (Robin/author)
W (Witness)

3

"I hope I'm strong enough to follow the law": Emotion and Objectivity in Capital Jurors' Decisions

AFTER LOCATING FORMER CAPITAL JURORS' names in public trial records, I sent letters to them asking for participation in my research. The letters explained my project and asked the jurors to contact me in order to be interviewed. Although many of my letters were ignored, some reached willing participants who called me and agreed to be interviewed. One letter, however, spurred a voicemail left on my phone by an irate husband. I have since erased it, but I remember its content and force. He condemned me for traumatizing his wife—the former juror—by sending the letter and for prolonging an enormously traumatic process that she thought was over with. He threatened that if I contacted his wife again by any means he would take action against me. I did not pursue that individual juror further.

This vignette is not presented as a request for sympathy or as a complaint, but as a vivid example of the intense emotional experience that serving as a juror on a capital trial is for many people. As we see in this husband's response to my request to his wife, capital trials, not surprisingly, are emotionally laden events for offenders and decision-makers alike. But jurors nonetheless feel pressure from both explicit and implicit legal ideologies that claim that emotion has no legitimate place in the law (e.g., Bandes 1996, 1999 Nussbaum 2004; Madeira 2012, 136–138). In my fieldwork experiences, while jurors recognized and relied upon emotions from defendants and witnesses during trial, they generally considered their *own* emotions irrelevant and harmful to their decisions. Criminal law designates certain emotional responses as reasonable and others as outside its purview (Nussbaum 2004). It would seem from my research that from *whom* the emotion is generated is an important factor in determining which emotions are sanctioned.

This chapter addresses an ambiguity, a paradox even, concerning the proper role of emotion in death penalty law and practice. Through judges' and attorneys' language and written instructions, jurors are urged, as they would be in any criminal trial, to remain unbiased and objective when arriving at a verdict. They hear this especially in the first stage of trial, during which they decide guilt or innocence. However, because the death penalty is an irreversible sanction, jurors are also told that their sentencing decisions are subjective and moral, and that they should consider the defendant as a unique individual.[1] Importantly, these instructions were often read as mutually exclusive. "Objective" decision-making, for which these jurors strove, meant – both

---

1. *Woodson v. North Carolina*, 428 U.S. 280 (1976).

to them and to some attorneys – forsaking their emotional judgments and reactions when coming to a verdict.[2]

This chapter demonstrates that many jurors, attorneys, and judges believe in, or at least act as if they believe in, a dichotomy between emotion and objectivity in law. While they recognize the degree to which "emotion pervades the law" (Bandes 1999, 1), jurors assert that the law tells them to eschew emotional considerations when making their decisions.[3] There are two problems with this, however. First, the Supreme Court, as will be described in more detail below, says that death is different. Post-*Furman* decisions have ruled that capital sentences should be individual, moral decisions, and jurors must therefore engage in *both* rational fact-finding and subjective considerations. Moreover, neuroscience, psychology, and related fields increasingly show that emotions are an integral component of what we think of as rational cognitive processes (e.g., Damasio 1994). Despite these factors, many of the jurors I studied relied on ideologies that equated just decisions with a lack of emotional input.

The analyses in this chapter unearth ways in which jurors used authoritative legal discourse, such as jury charges and judges' words, as well as ideologies of reason, objectivity, and truth, often couched in talk about "evidence," to counter the intersubjective, emotional moments they experienced during trials. The Supreme Court's efforts to promote capital sentencing decisions that are moral and individual has led, I argue, not to more just decisions, but rather to deny capital defendants the full consideration the law requires. I argue

2. For a more thorough discussion of this paradox in jury instructions, see Conley Riner 2017..

3. See the 2006 special issue of *Law and Human Behavior* 30, no 2, on emotion and legal decision-making for a thorough review of this topic.

further that the ways in which emotionality and objectivity were manipulated by attorneys and judges during death penalty voir dire frequently resulted in creating not only death-*qualified*, but death-*inclined*, juries.

DEFINING EMOTION AND EMPATHY

This chapter focuses on emotion in capital jurors' decisions, but it and the following two chapters also engage a related phenomenon, empathy, which has received significant attention in death penalty and other legal research. While emotion and empathy are related concepts, they are not identical, and they are frequently presented in legal research as self-evident and thus left undefined. It is therefore worth briefly parsing them for analytic clarity.

Emotion in legal decision-making and other legal processes has been approached primarily from psychological and philosophical perspectives. Among these approaches, there is little consensus on a single definition, and, as Susan Bandes (1999) writes in her introduction to an edited volume on law and emotion, "It is error of a sort to assume a blanket definition of any emotion" (13), as "how we define emotion may, legitimately, depend on why we need to know" (12). This book is dedicated, as indicated in the introduction, to explaining how capital jurors understand their tasks, and I therefore rely in part on their formulations of emotion for my working definition.

I present here an excerpt from one juror's interview, in which he reflected on the complex issue of emotions and their role in his jury's verdict. I had asked him about how his jury came to a consensus, and his discussion of how the jury worked through an initial stalemate led to his comments about emotion.

> Some of the feelings that people had on both sides were *strictly emotional type feelings.* Because when you'd be questioned on it, they'd realize well, *I don't really have a <u>reason</u>.* I mean there's not anything in the evidence that I can point to that says, here's the reason I believe this. *This is just kind of a feeling I have.* And it, I think it made people question themselves more and look at things more. 'Cause I know a couple times, once during the guilt or innocence, you know, somebody said, Well what, what did they say in there that made you feel this way? Well, you know, I don't really know anything that made me feel this way. I just did and, then they start looking back through the evidence and they realize that, well, *maybe this is just an emotional feeling* and I really don't have anything to base it on. And judging by the evidence, because you read the charge, it said you can't use sympathy or compassion, intuition, or any of these other things. *Well, we're all made of all that stuff.* You're gonna use it. You can't not use it. And *it's hard to get that analytical about a man's life.* And not just his life but his family, the people that are gonna have to be incarcerated with him, the people that are gonna have to be guarding him, all that. *You can't take emotion out of it totally.*

This juror's reflection expresses a view of emotion common to Anglo-American law: emotion and reason are separate processes, and emotion is less legitimate in a trial context. His repeated reference to "just" a feeling reveals this view of emotion as a frivolous distraction to jurors' decisions. In the end, though, the juror admits that emotion is "what we're all made of," and it therefore necessarily informed his decision. His ruminations indicate that the law nonetheless wants jurors to be "analytical" about their decisions, which confounds this juror to a certain degree, especially when a man's life is at stake. This book's discussion of emotion focuses on its purported status as a bodily, fallible, private phenomenon, set apart from reason and rational thought. This conceptualization resonates with legal ideologies in which emotions are treated as "antithetical to order, justice, and coherence" (Laster and O'Malley 1996, 24). I argue, however, that emotions in fact play a central role in social judgments of all kinds and are indispensable to cognitive processes (e.g., Helion and Pizarro 2013; Lerner and Keltner 2000; 2001; Damasio 2008). This perspective shifts the focus from emotions as "fixed and internal states" to "dynamic processes that shape and are shaped by social and institutional context" (Bandes 2008a, 388).

In legal scholarship, definitions of empathy are similarly elusive. This book relies on a definition of empathy developed by Husserl (1989), Stein (1989), and subsequently Throop (2008; 2010; see also Hollan and Throop 2008), according to which empathy is humans' ability to approximate others' subjective experiences through our own embodied experiences. When I see someone in pain, for instance, I have some understanding of what that feels like, given that I, too, have experienced pain. In this conceptualization, empathy and emotion, while not identical phenomena, operate in close relation. Empathy is "informed by the work of emotions" (Throop 2010, 772); one is often primed to the experience of another through emotion (Throop 2010, 772). Testimony in court that is particularly experientially intense, for example, or pictures that engender highly emotional responses from jurors may stand out among their experiences more than the textual forms of evidence that the law privileges (cf. Fishfader et al. 1996). For this reason, defense attorneys often object, with frequent success, to saturating jurors with pictures of crime scenes and victims' dead bodies as prejudicial to their defendants. As the analyses below demonstrate, jurors regard empathy, just as they do emotion, as an experience that should not inform their decisions in capital trials.

INSTRUCTING CAPITAL JURORS: A CONTRADICTION

The ambiguity concerning emotion in law is highlighted in death penalty trials, in which subjective feelings about individuals on trial for their lives clash against restrictive legal rules that attempt to reduce these experiences to objective fact-finding. This ambiguity is further compounded by the bifurcated structure of the capital trial. The idea of juror impartiality (Gobert 1988), in particular, becomes especially problematic in death penalty trials because jurors have to be two kinds of decision-makers. During the culpability phase, they take on the role of fact-finder, just as they would in any other criminal case. The sentencing phase, however, is different. First, because the death penalty is irreversible, jurors' fact-finding duties come under greater scrutiny. Capital defendants must be protected against arbitrary sentences; consequently, jurors are repeatedly instructed that they must remain impartial and unbiased in rendering their verdicts, and, above all, follow the law (Weisberg 1983).

During sentencing phase deliberations, however, jurors are also asked to evaluate defendants in a qualitatively different way than when deciding guilt. Because of the severity of the death penalty, the Supreme Court has avowed that each defendant's life should be considered individually (*Woodson v. North Carolina*, 428 U.S. 280 (1976)), including his character and background (presented in the trial as mitigating evidence), before a death sentence can be given. Empathy is arguably an integral part of this process of individualization, as it requires jurors to conceptualize and judge an other's experiences (Henderson 1987, 1650). The Supreme Court decision in *Penry v. Lynaugh* (492 U.S. 302 (1989)), which established the second special issue question as it now stands, solidified the "fundamental difference" between culpability and sentencing decisions (Vartkessian, Sorensen, and Kelly 2014, 7). The decision urges jurors not to regard a sentencing deliberation as a "factual undertaking," but, rather, as a consideration of the defendant's "moral blameworthiness" (Vartkessian, Sorensen, and Kelly 2014, 7). The capital sentencing decision has been further categorized in case law as a personal, "moral judgment" (U.S. vs. Wilson, 2013). This "death is different" quality of capital trials requires jurors to render a decision on an "intensely moral, subjective matter" that defies legal rules (Weisberg 1983, 308). The requirement to consider the individual morality of the defendant flies in the face of well-established legal ideologies that decision-making should be objective and based merely on facts.

Capital jury instructions reflect the contradictory requirements of capital jurors. Jurors' charges send conflicting messages as to whether they should consider emotion and related experiences in their decisions. There are no required jury instructions in Texas capital cases, but those I observed used very similar punishment charges, based both on pattern instructions and attorneys' suggestions. I present below excerpts from the punishment charge in the Lewis case as an

example; it is fairly representative of most other charges I
reviewed:

> The jury shall consider *all evidence admitted* during this trial,
> including evidence of the Defendant's background or character
> or the circumstances of the offense. . . . You are further instructed
> that you are *not to be swayed by mere sentiment, conjecture, sym-*
> *pathy, passion, prejudice,* public opinion or public feeling in con-
> sidering all of the evidence before you. . . . the jury shall consider
> *all evidence admitted* at trial . . . including the circumstances of
> the offense, the defendant's character and background, and the
> *personal moral culpability of the defendant.* . . . the jury is in-
> structed to consider mitigating evidence to be evidence that a
> juror might regard as reducing the defendant's *moral blamewor-*
> *thiness.* You are to deliberate *only on the evidence that is properly*
> *before you* in this trial and to give this case individual delibera-
> tion based on *only the evidence admitted* before you in this trial.
> You are instructed that it is *only from the witness stand that the*
> *jury is permitted to receive evidence* regarding this case. . . . the
> answers to the Special Issues must be determined and agreed
> upon by each juror on *the facts of the case,* as testified by the wit-
> nesses, and the law as given in the Charge of the Court.

The overall message of these instructions is equivocal. On
one hand, jurors are reminded again and again that they may
only consider "evidence" and "facts" when deciding on a punishment. According to multiple jurors, as we will see below,
this implies that jurors' subjective considerations, as well witnesses and defendants' emotions, should not be included.

This is reinforced by the so-called no-sympathy clause,
which instructs that "sentiment[s]"—including "sympathy"
and "passion"—should not impact jurors' decisions.[4] Several

---

4. Use of this clause in capital sentencing instructions was challenged in *Cali-*
fornia v. Brown, 479 U.S. 538 (1987), but it was held to be constitutional.

defense attorneys pushed for the addition of this clause to penalty phase instructions because they feared jurors' sympathy for victims' families would drive them to impose a death sentence. In the end, however, jurors used such verbiage to deny sympathy with *defendants* and justify a sentence of death.[5] Thus, when jurors were instructed to refrain from allowing feelings such as sympathy into their decisions, they tended to generalize this to mean that only aspects of testimony that could be categorized as "evidence" and "facts" could be considered in their sentencing decisions. According to these sections of their instructions, jurors are "to rely on testimony and exhibits presented during the trial insofar as they relate to specific, rationally-described, non-emotional aggravating and mitigating circumstances" (Cobb 1989, 396).

On the other hand, jurors are instructed that their sentencing decision is a "moral" one, and specifically that evidence considered may include the "personal, moral culpability" of the defendant. This aspect of juror's sentencing decisions, though required by the Supreme Court to be included in their instructions, was downplayed among the jurors I spoke with in comparison to the directives to allow nothing beyond the "evidence" and "facts of the case" to impact their decisions. The Supreme Court has also permitted jurors to consider mercy in their decisions to sentence someone to death (*Morgan v. Illinois*, 504 U.S. 719, 739 (1992)), which, at least in lay terminology (and mercy is not legally defined), requires a compassionate

---

5. *California v. Brown* addressed this very issue. The opinion argued that the sympathy clause only denied that jurors may rely on sympathetic feelings that were not "tethered" to the mitigating evidence presented. Dissenters argued, as I do here, that jurors do not understand the nuance of this instruction and instead read it as barring all sympathetic feeling from their decisions (see Nussbaum 2004, 52–56 for a discussion of this decision).

appeal to another's experience (Sarat 2005). The law remains ambivalent, too, on its stance toward mercy, sometimes ruling the supposed capriciousness of mercy too detrimental to be allowed in legal judgments (Garvey 1996; see also Cobb 1989). In capital sentencing instructions, the second special issue, or "mitigation," question attempts to promote a subjective form of decision-making, in which the defendant's individuality and morality should be considered above all else. It does not include a burden of proof and is much more open-ended in terms of what kinds of evidence jurors are instructed to consider than the first special issue. This evidence is rarely explicitly delineated, however. In one exception, drawn from a 2008 case in which the defendant received LWOP, the charge directed as follows:

> A mitigating circumstance may include, but is not limited to any aspect of the defendant's character, background, record, *emotional stability or instability* . . . which you believe make a death sentence inappropriate.

This charge addresses emotion specifically, instructing jurors to consider as evidence more subjective phenomena than they may have otherwise considered.

SOCIALIZING JURORS INTO FACT-FINDERS: CAPITAL VOIR DIRE

When capital jurors discussed their experiences with me, there was often an undercurrent of frustration. For many of them, serving on a capital jury inflicted more than the usual inconvenience associated with jury service; it was a tremendous emotional burden with which a large percentage continued to struggle at the time of their interviews. Many of them experienced frustration stemming from what they perceived as a lack of guidance during their trials. The state was asking them to do something almost unthinkable, and telling them very little about how to do it. As one juror relayed to me:

> Let me just tell you [long pause] you know, maybe (admit) there's a lot of tension there and [pause] you are looking for a, you know, a life raft somewhere to just guide you, help you, because this is a very difficult question that you're answering, in terms of emotional as well as just, not just intellectual. And, you know, it was very dissatisfying that we couldn't get, you know, anything from clarification to explanations, anything like that. Now I understood it intellectually, but, man, that put us in a really tough situation.

Despite this frustration, the jurors with whom I spoke were dedicated to serving well. Jurors' assumptions about emotion and law often came through when reflecting on what it meant to be a good juror. Overall, I found that "following the law"—and all that entails—was valued in capital jury service over any other quality. Good capital jurors were people who claimed they could put their own beliefs, values, and perspectives aside in the name of "the law" (Haney 1997). This runs contrary, however, to the claim that jurors should provide a cross-section of opinions based on each juror's individual background (Appleman 2009; Chibundu 2008). Texas capital jurors tended to focus on the former understanding of juries, based on notions of rational, unbiased decision-making (Landsman 2002). In capital trials, I argue, jurors relied on this idea—conveyed in the form of authoritative legal language—that they should separate their trial decisions from their own experiences. This often served to justify their decisions for death.

In addition to receiving their explicit instructions, jurors inferred ways to theorize their sentencing decisions by engaging in courtroom interactions (Ochs 2002). During voir dire in particular, jurors are socialized into their roles in the legal system. They learn, among other things, their obligations, what actions are valued or condemned in court, and how to think and talk like a juror. The voir dire process, therefore, does not *select* jurors, but *creates* them (Balch et al. 1976, 280).

Attorneys' and judges' talk during voir dire often complicated the conflicting instructions regarding emotion that jurors were faced with. Jurors consistently heard, from voir dire onward, that their decisions were to be based on facts and evidence and should not be influenced by anything from the "outside" or by their feelings or emotions. These voir dire messages inspire an ideology of determinism, facticity, and objectivity (cf. Mertz 2007), which leads jurors to believe that their individual feelings are irrelevant to and should be banished from their decision-making.

The following examples are excerpted from individual voir dire questioning sessions in multiple cases, during which potential jurors were extensively questioned one by one by both the prosecutors and defense attorneys. In the first example, a prosecutor's question takes the form of a statement, through which he essentially instructs the potential juror about her duty:

P: We're not telling people they can't have emotion, but you make your call based on the facts.

J: Whatever the law *dictates*.

While the prosecutor explicitly permits the admission of emotion in jurors' decisions, his prompt opposes "facts," the sine qua non for legal trials, to emotional considerations, thereby denigrating the status of the latter. The potential juror concurs, understanding this as obligated by the law.

I have stated above that, at least in the abstract, theorists recognize emotions as integral to intellectual processes such as judgment. How, then, do jurors propose to rid their decision-making of this purportedly integral component? Judges and attorneys often directed them in this regard, telling them that all they must do is put their emotion and any other extrafactual thought, belief, or feeling aside and "follow the law." Despite legal warnings against relying on any personal feelings, jurors were often informed during voir dire that they necessarily bring with them into the courtroom their own experiences and knowledge that would undoubtedly inform their decisions. A judge in one case told jurors during jury selection, "We come in here with lifetime experience," which "leaves us with certain impressions, leaves marks on us." They were always told in the end, however, that these personal considerations must be set aside in order for them to serve as jurors.

Jurors often reiterated this spatial trope of putting feelings "aside." Even if they came into voir dire with reportedly strong feelings about the death penalty, once asked by attorneys if they could eschew them to follow the law, they tended to acquiesce. This assumption constitutes a dichotomous relationship between emotion and objectivity, often assumed in Anglo-American law, in which the absence of one equals the presence of another. In the following excerpts, a defense attorney questioned potential jurors about feelings they had identified as bringing with them into the courtroom.

> D: Could you put your *feelings* of the father of the victim *aside*?
>
> J: Yes. I would like to think I could be that *objective*.
>
> D: If we keep you on this jury, will you still be a 10 [on a scale of 1–10 in which 10 indicates strong support for the death penalty]?
>
> J: It's my *personal belief*, but following *the law, I would follow it.*

The emotion-objectivity dichotomy is clearly established in this example. Though he had yet to see any written instructions, this potential juror seemed to understand—from his oral directions from judges and questioning by attorneys—that "personal" considerations, such as "beliefs" and "feelings," must be set aside in order to make their decisions and be "objective." One of the jurors I interviewed reiterated strongly this stance on his decision during a post-trial interview:

> Whatever the state asks, I'm going to rigidly abide by it. And *I'm going to form my opinions by what the state asked me to do.* And if we get to the question phase, I'm going to answer those questions honestly. I'm going to *put aside what I kind of think should happen.*

Thus despite rulings that define a capital decision as a "personal, moral judgment," many jurors with whom I spoke and those potential jurors I observed during voir dire understood their duty to mean that their personal, individual beliefs and feelings should not constitute part of their decisions.

OBJECTIVITY AND IMPARTIAL JURIES

Talking with jurors about what their service meant to them uncovered some of the symbolic discourses with which they conceptualized the purpose of juries overall. One of the more prominent tropes was that jurors should be "objective." In academic circles, the meaning of objectivity has been thoroughly debated in the last century (e.g., Rorty 1995). In the context of capital trials, objectivity seemed to take on a specific connotation. Specifically, the notion of impartiality—the lack of bias or prejudice—was equated with conceptions of objectivity.

Both scholarly definitions and jurors' own conceptions of impartiality and objectivity can be sourced to Enlightenment notions of scientific proof and rationality. In line with Enlightenment ideologies, much legal theory and law and society research posits a contrastive relationship between reason and emotion, even if to promote the latter in legal and deliberative contexts (e.g., Ryfe 2002). Rational deliberation, one of the core facets of liberal democracies, is often hailed as an achievement of reason over emotion, thus theoretically eluding biased judgment. Impartiality is similarly deemed by the public to require an eschewal of emotionality for reason (Krause 2011, 100). Good jurors, in this sense, embody "distance and dispassion" (Abramson 2000, 21) in their decisions.[6]

For Texas capital jurors, being objective encompassed an array of related concepts, including fairness, honesty, and reliance on evidence. In the following interview

---

6. This topic will be reviewed further in chapter 4.

excerpt, I asked one juror directly about what his role meant
to him:

> R: What do you think just the role of a jury is in a trial
> (like this) I mean, if I were to say, why do we have
> juries to decide this kind of thing?
>
> J: To give an *objective*, you know, an *objective feeling* on
> the crime and the suitable punishment. You know it's,
> you can't have a judge do it. You can't have just one
> person do it because *you don't have enough people
> where someone, one person could be a past victim of a
> similar crime*, you know, so it *gives someone the most
> fair opportunity that they could possibly have.* If you
> had a judge handing out punishments that saw capital
> murders, you know, three days a week, they, I mean
> they're smart enough that they would try not to
> become, you know, desensitized to it, but they would
> be, you know. So *giving someone an honest, objective
> chance, at a proper punishment.*

Objectivity appears repeatedly in this juror's response. Echo-
ing the spirit of the Sixth Amendment, this juror conceives
objectivity as achieved through the jury as a collectivity. Relying on only one decision-maker, he explained, could result
in a biased decision if that person had a particular perspective on the crime, for instance. With many jurors, however,
this bias is potentially canceled out so that the defendant may
have a fair trial.

During voir dire, judges often reiterated the duty of a
jury as achieving objective decision-making. During his first
address to the jury panel of over two hundred venire persons,

one judge described to the group how Texas jurors are meant to conduct themselves. His notion of objectivity, also embedded in Enlightenment ideologies, rests on the eradication of supposedly subjective determinations:

> The first thing we know is juries in the State of Texas do not go out and deliberate and *subjectively* determine, we'll give this defendant life in this case. We'll give that defendant death in that case. Instead, what *we* do is *we* have juries make *objective* findings as to what the *evidence* is.

In his address, another theme emerges regarding jury decision-making and objectivity. Being objective means relying on evidence alone, he explained, while decisions based on any other considerations are deemed subjective and thus not applicable in a trial context. This form of objectivity, he asserts, is what he and the state of Texas require.

The pursuit of objectivity in jury decision-making includes not only eschewing emotion, but also suppressing any subjective considerations—what is inside the "individual mind." This resonates with historical accounts of the origin of the jury, which describe its purpose as democratically representing collective or community values. Thus, as a juror, some argue, one suppresses the "I" in reverence for the "we"; deliberation, jury scholars argue, transforms individual biases. The decision-making body of twelve is designed so that lay judges' perspectives will be dispersed across the group (Abramson 2000).

The following examples illustrate metaphors of the individual mind used as explanation for how legal objectivity can be achieved. Below, a venire person explains during individual voir dire questioning her process of making a decision about guilt:

> J: My *mind might say* if you're charged with it, you're guilty, but *the law says* innocence.... I think that there's a reason he's been charged with two murders . . . *what I believe in my mind.* But I have to listen to both sides.

The prosecutor later asks this same person,

> P: Is this blemish *just in your mind*?
> J: Yes.

Both of these excerpts deal with the tricky issue of jurors bringing their own experiences and viewpoints into trial with them, again part of why lay juries were formed in the first place. This potential juror was taught during voir dire, however, that what is "in [her] mind" should be put aside to make room for the law.

In the following, a potential juror was questioned by a defense attorney about the future danger question:

> D: Would you automatically *think* someone convicted of capital murder is a future danger?
> J: I lean towards yes because there's a tendency there, so, I'd at least *think* that.... I'd have the tendency to *think that in my mind* . . . [but] I would still need to *be proved* that he is a threat.

Again, we see that what is in the mind can be set aside so that proof in the form of facts can be relied on in jurors' decisions. Not all jurors admit to the ease of setting thoughts aside, however.

Another defense attorney asked a related question to a potential juror, but to a different end, remarking that ignoring what's in your mind is not such an easy task:

> D: Your beliefs *don't leave your head*, do they?
> J: No. Not about the death penalty.

This juror explains that these beliefs that exist in his head couldn't be set aside, even if he were chosen for the jury. Again, we see evidence here that setting beliefs aside, separating yourself from what exists in your mind, cannot always be trumped by the objectivity of the law. Nonetheless, what it means to be a juror seems to have morphed since the American jury was first constituted, at least in the context of death penalty cases. Being a juror now seems to be about forging oneself during voir dire into a blank slate upon which facts and evidence can be etched. This includes somehow separating oneself from his or her individual mind in order to join the collective, another remnant of Enlightenment thinking. How a death penalty juror can make an "individual, moral judgment" given these criteria is left in question.

POWER OF THE JUDGE

As allowed in the Federal Rules of Criminal Procedure (Rule 47(a)), judges may question venire persons during voir dire (see Stanley 1977). While potential jurors are already in vulnerable positions during capital voir dire, sitting in the witness stand answering often quite personal questions, the direct questioning of a judge can exacerbate the intimidating nature of the interaction. As Bourdieu (1979, 83) writes in his discussion of symbolic power, "The power of words and commands, the power of words to give orders and bring order, lies in belief in the legitimacy of the words and of the person who utters them, a belief which words themselves cannot produce." This power asymmetry is exacerbated by the interactional power differential between questioner and respondent, according to which those answering questions in conversation often feel compelled to please the questioner (Amsterdam and Bruner 2009). Additionally, it is generally considered face-threatening and is thus dispreferred (Pomerantz 1984), in the conversational sense, to disagree with a person of relative authority. Thus when the language of objectivity discussed above is coupled with the power of the judge himself delivering the message to be objective, jurors are often left with no choice but to agree that objectivity rules in the court of law. Even when not explicitly recognized by jurors, judges can have tremendous impact on how jurors see their duties as described during voir dire, and on whether they are eventually qualified or not.

The following examples reveal jurors' recognition that the judge, or court, serves as an additional layer of authority urging them to remain "objective" and set their own beliefs and emotions aside, even when they are reminded that they are asked to make individual moral judgments. In the following excerpt from a defense attorney's questioning, the venire person defines his *moral* duty as being *objective*. The venire person, moreover, describes his morally just decision as following what the "court" directs him to do.

> J: Based on the evidence I've heard, my *moral decision* is to follow the lead on *what the court instructs me to do.*
>
> D: It's going to be a *moral decision* on your part. . . .

J: I realize that would be a difficult one. I don't know, *I hope I can remain objective.*

As I often observed during individual voir dire questioning, many jurors gave conflicting answers to the prosecution and defense attorneys, at which point judges intervened in order to get the "real" answer. Interactions of this kind often consisted of a death penalty-prone juror stating to the prosecutor that he or she could put aside a belief that anyone convicted of capital murder should get the death penalty and follow the law, basing the decision merely on the facts presented. Then, when questioned by the defense, the same juror stated that if the accused were found guilty of capital murder, the juror would always give the death penalty.

In the following example, a potential juror told the prosecutor that he could "keep his mind open" to both a death and a life sentence. This metaphor of an open mind is often used to convey to jurors that individual bias should be set aside. The juror later expressed to the defense attorneys a belief that the death penalty should be given for anyone convicted of capital murder and that a life sentence without parole does not make sense as an available punishment. He stated to the defense attorney:

J: I think if we're gonna say you can't walk around free as part of society until your natural death, then you shouldn't have that, you should get the death penalty.

D: Then you come into the penalty phase with those beliefs?

J: Yes.

D: If your moral belief is such that people deserve death, then how can you make a *moral judgment* for life?

J: If no *evidence is presented* against it [life/death?], then
      I think it's the obvious answer.

The juror had thus told the prosecutor that he could keep his
mind open to both punishment options, and then told the
defense that his mind would essentially be made up after a
capital murder conviction. The judge then interjected in an
attempt to clear up the contradictions. Upon being addressed
by the judge, the juror swiveled his chair to face the bench
and looked up to engage the judge's eye contact:

C: Let me interrupt. You have an *opinion* of the death
      penalty. By the way, *you don't have to agree with me.*
      If you come down to question two, mitigation, will
      you *search your heart* to answer the question? This is
      where the rubber meets the road. Will you be more
      influenced to say that's not mitigating because of
      your belief about the death penalty than if you had a
      neutral belief?
J: I don't think my prior *opinion* is going to push it to *the
      other side.*
C: You're able to *categorize things in your mind* and just
      consider what's *in front of you?*
J: Yes.

The judge, to his credit, attempted to dispel potential intimi-
dation caused by his position of power, assuring the juror he
did not have to agree with him. Despite their good intentions, jurors often changed their answers when confronted
by judges. Some were reduced to tears when faced with addressing them directly. The judge in the example above began
by highlighting the opinions, feelings, and individual beliefs

that any juror brings into the courtroom, using such emotional, metaphoric language as "searching your heart." In the end, however, he subtly suggested that jurors should have neutral beliefs when coming to trial. The venire person and judge continued to speak of neutrality in spatial terms: what is in the mind should be put aside in heed of physical evidence, positioned in front of the juror in the courtroom. After this question exchange with the judge, the juror was qualified, requiring the defense to use a peremptory strike on him.

OATH, HONESTY, AND OBLIGATION

In addition to being influenced by the rhetorical sway of language of objectivity and judges' and attorneys' orders to follow the law, jurors expressed that it is their obligation, based on the oath they take, to put aside their emotion and individual opinions in order to be fair and impartial jurors. Embedded in this obligation to the juror's oath is a trust in truth and honesty. Though legal scholars recognize the partial and multiple nature of legal truths, attorneys and judges often tell jurors that their job is "decide what the truth is." In the following example, a venire person expressed fear to the prosecutor that she wouldn't be able to decide someone's fate, that it would be "too emotional." She then assured him, when asked if she could answer the punishment question leading to a death sentence, "I mean, if I'm under oath to tell the truth I could answer yes to that."

The potential juror later reiterated to the defense attorney that she worried she could not give the death penalty for fear it would spur an emotional breakdown. After this vacillation, the judge questioned her, using honesty as bait for her to agree that she could be a fair juror. She had already begun crying when the judge asked her to turn her chair toward him:

> C: *The law* kind of puts you in a bad situation, so don't let me upset you. There's a little bit of a conflict, so you have to tell me which way it really is. If you say no to mitigation, then a death sentence will be carried out. Would you give *true answers or possibly falsify them*?
>
> J: I would give true answers.
>
> C: You understand no is a death sentence? *You take an oath . . .*
>
> J: Yes, judge, I'll give true answers *so help me God. I'd have to, yes.*
>
> C: Could you take that oath? Could you do that?
>
> J: Yes.
>
> C: *You promise me* you'd give true answers to the questions? Without regard to what happens to him?
>
> J: I want to think that I'd be strong enough to do that because *I'm a truthful person.*
>
> C: Will you or will you not?
>
> J: I will.

After attempting to ameliorate the intimidating circumstances of the encounter, the judge came close to bullying this juror into being qualified. He informed the woman that after the inconsistent answers she gave the attorneys, he would discover which way it "really is." Next, he challenged her allegiance to the truth and to her oath, asking if she would falsify her answers, to which she not surprisingly answered no. She regurgitated some of the language of the oath to assure the judge of her honesty, "so help me God." The judge continued, asking for a personal promise that the juror would give true answers; she affirmed that she would. Despite the her concerns that she could not actually give a death sentence, the language of truth and obligation, coupled with the powerful position of the judge, won out and the juror was qualified. In this case, the state used a peremptory strike.

JURORS' POSTVERDICT COMMENTS ON EMOTION AND OBJECTIVITY

Despite the Supreme Court's insistence that death penalty jurors must make two qualitatively different decisions in the culpability and punishment deliberations, jurors with whom I spoke did not distinguish their two phases of deliberations in this way. Many jurors interpreted their instructions, rather, as barring them from considering any kind of emotion in both their culpability and sentencing deliberations, and thus as instructing them only to rely on "evidence" and "facts." A lengthy section from an interview with Jed, a jury foreman, exemplifies this perspective. I had not asked him directly about emotion at this point in the interview. My questions leading up to his response were regarding specific words used in his jury charge, such as "continuing threat" and "reasonable doubt." He told me that when his jury was considering these issues during the punishment phase, it was the jury charge that "swung the case," a comment on which I asked him to elaborate.

In his response, he recounted that particular parts of his instructions directed him to bar emotional experience from his considerations, despite additional instructions to the contrary. He recounted testimony from the sentencing phase of his trial, during which the defendant's father was brought to the stand and pleaded with the jury not to execute his son. Jed reflected on this father's emotional testimony and struggled with how to fit his *own* experience of the testimony into his decision-making.

J: That was what swung the case.

R: What was what swung the case?

J: What the jury, what our jury charge, what our charge was.

R: So can you explain?

J: You want me to elaborate?

R: Yes, please.

J: Okay. As you can imagine, any case like this deals a lot with emotion. In other words, I am fairly unemotional, but it is very difficult to *sit there and listen to someone's gray-haired old daddy beg you not to kill their boy* and try to take blame for the way he turned out, and you know, he may be right. However, the charge specif—that we as jurors, every one of us, swore to, on the day of our oath, the charge said that we would only let evidence guide us. We would not let supposition, emotion, prejudice, I forget the other term, but something like that, okay? So, you must try to *put your emotion aside* as much as you can and *only go on what is presented as evidence, either from the stand or physical evidence.*

R: Right.

J: And when you couple that with, well, I said I would do it, *I swore I would do it, by honor I've got to do it.* As much as I hate to do it, I've got to do it. Because that's what I said I would do. And this is the *evidence* we have.

R: Do you think that was hard for a lot of jurors? To do?

J: Hm?

R: Do you think that was hard for a lot of jurors?

J: Oh yes! Of course it's always hard, hard for anybody. Especially given some of the jurors that we had. . . .

R: So how, how do you think people sort of, you or other jurors, put their emotion aside and you know, what were, how did they actually do that?

J: Well, when you go down, you had to go again, *you had to go by what, what we knew.* Not what we supposed, not what we guessed, not what we wished, but what we knew. . . .

R: Do you remember a specific, I mean you don't have to, you know, talk about specific conversations, but just, were, did people say, you know was there someone getting emotional and then someone else said, no here you have to look at the evi—you know was there that, kind of?

J: Nothing that harsh, but again, myself [and] several others have, would have to say, or would have to make a statement like, well, yeah, maybe, *but that's not what the evidence shows.* Well yeah, true, he didn't, you know, he uh, he had a bad childhood. Yes, but, everybody in this room's had bad things happen to them. And they didn't kill anybody. You know, everybody has had periods in their life that were terrible. And you wouldn't wish them on anybody. But that's not an excuse, unless you're mentally incompetent. So that was brought up over and over and over and over and over. I'm sure to some ad nauseum [laughing] you know. But (), that's when I said, you have to *get your emotion out of it as much as you can.* Because yeah, he had a tough life. He had a hard life as a kid. But if we went on that, then that would be an excuse for anybody to do anything. You can't do that. You can't suppose that.

Jed's recollection of a father's testimony illustrates a phenomenological shift many jurors underwent regarding their trial experiences. Even for such an unemotional man as himself, he explained, it was extremely difficult to have been present with someone begging him not to kill his son. Jed was nonetheless able to put this emotional experience aside, he asserted, and not let it affect his decision, as this is what he believed his instructions directed him to do. The authority of his jury charge and oath, specifically, reportedly allowed him to remove himself from the experiential reality of the trial in order to make what he believed to be the right kind of legal decision.

Similar to venire persons quoted above, he cited his oath as the authority for his proclamation: "I swore I would do it, by honor I've got to do it." He also framed his dedication to bar emotion in moral terms—it was an act of honor. When I then asked him if this was a hard process for jurors to undergo, he conceded that it was very hard, especially for "certain jurors," by which he was referring primarily to women. His explanation for how jurors put emotion aside, despite the difficulty of the task, reflects the legal ideologies of objectivity described above, in which what one "knows" is opposed to what one feels. His reference to "certain jurors," moreover, reveals values inherent to this ideology that pose rationality as an attribute of primarily white, well-educated males (Adler and Peirce 1993), as those "certain jurors" were female. He additionally cited "evidence" as the opposing and preferred information to rely on in his jury's decision, rather than emotion or other similar considerations. He and other jurors, he reported, used a discourse of evidence to convince fellow jurors that emotion should not be a factor in their decisions.

Especially telling in this passage is Jed's elaboration on this issue, which includes citing multiple forms of mitigating evidence. It is precisely in regards to mitigating evidence that jurors are required to make individual, moral decisions, to be something other than fact-finders. This jury's conflation of its duties during culpability and punishment phase deliberations, as well as its reliance on an unrealistic separation of emotion and rationality, kept the jurors from being the kinds of jurors the Supreme Court has required.

Throughout the interviews I conducted, many jurors highlighted emotions overall and the perceived need to "put emotion aside" in their deliberations, in both culpability and sentencing phases. Various tropes were used to describe the mechanisms by which they did this. Jed's formulation closely parallels Enlightenment discourse relied on in law that reifies an opposition between emotion and knowledge:

> R: So how do you think people sort of, you or other jurors *put their emotion aside* and, you know, what were, how did they actually do that?
>
> J: Well, when you go down, you had to go again, *you had to go by what, what we knew. Not what we supposed, not what we guessed, not what we wished, but what we knew.*

My question here included repetition of Jed's language from earlier in the interview that putting emotion aside was a requisite duty of jurors. His subsequent response is illuminating; he identified the emotion-resistant force as what he *knew*. Packed in with emotion, on the other side of this opposition, were supposition, guessing, and wishing. This juror thus constructed an ideology in which emotion is equated with unreliable, even fanciful, modes of thought, all of which are subordinated to "knowledge" in the context of deliberations.

Jurors often spoke in their interviews of the difficulty of putting personal feelings aside, despite their beliefs that the law called for it. Prior to the following excerpt I asked a juror if there were any "concerns beyond the evidence" that affected his punishment decision. His response was that his biggest concern was his personal prejudice, which he explained as follows:

> So, what part of that decision has to do with all *the things that I brought into the room, and how could I make just a flat factual decision here.* You know, how much do all the *filters of what I've known and experienced* to deal with that. That was a concern for me.

This juror recognized that he could not achieve the legal ideal of making a "flat, factual decision," but, rather, what he brought into the courtroom, including his own personal experiences, necessarily colored his decisions. This was his primary concern, however, revealing the pull he felt to set such personal considerations aside.

EMOTION AND MASCULINITY

While this book does not attempt to address fully the complexities of gender and emotion in legal contexts,[7] their

7. See Collier 2010 for an enlightening review.

undeniable interconnection requires some mention of the subject. Quoted above, Jed was the only juror who gave explicitly gendered comments about emotion and jury decision-making. It is true that those jurors who strongly reacted to my requests for interviews and either refused to participate or spoke with me begrudgingly tended to be women. Men with whom I spoke, however, often shared intense emotional experiences with me. The only juror to cry during an interview—publicly in a restaurant, moreover—was a man. And women and men alike displayed vitriolic responses to defendants' criminal actions.

I therefore remain hesitant to attribute any reliable patterns to the ways in which differently gendered jurors handled or interpreted emotions. I will share, however, a brief story about one defendant that sheds light on the deeply embedded notions of masculinity and emotion that undergird much of how criminal law is practiced (Baker 2005). In a medium-sized college town in east Texas, a young, white military combat veteran shot his ex-girlfriend and her brother to death in their home. His trial was fairly typical of the capital trials I observed throughout my time in Texas courtrooms: he was found guilty without much argument among jurors, his mitigation evidence included a record of mental illness, and he was sentenced to death. He was typical in another way as well. He expressed very little emotion during the trial, either visibly or verbally. He did not testify and his demeanor during the trial was described by his jurors as "blank" and uninvolved.

There was significant discussion among his two male attorneys whether he should testify. He was a young man with a fairly pleasant countenance when he engaged in normal conversation. However, his attorneys only wanted him to testify if he could display emotion on the stand—regret, sorrow, remorse, or something of the sort. I remember one particular discussion during a break in the trial, out of the presence of the defendant. His attorneys discussed whether he would be able cry on the stand, which they claimed would have been the most desirable outcome of his testimony. His lead attorney expressed real doubt that he would display emotion in the courtroom. His military background especially was raised as a barrier to his public expression of emotion. In the end, this defendant did not testify as per the advice of his lawyers. His attorneys assumed that his lack of emotional display may have been read by jurors as callousness or lack of remorse for his murders. My interviews with jurors, as examined in the next chapter, reveal this perspective to be quite accurate. Thus, while none of the responses from individual jurors nor any outcomes from individual cases led to a conclusion that gender could be singled out as a causative or correlative factor in death penalty decisions, jurors' and other legal actors' language during and after death penalty trials rested on ideologies that privilege a rational, and thus masculinized, subject in legal contexts.

PUTTING EMOTION ASIDE AND DEATH QUALIFICATION

This chapter has explored a small sample of the varied ways emotion is understood and treated in capital trials. From voir dire onward, jurors are inundated with discourses of objectivity that propose to allow one to "put emotion aside." During the jury selection process, those who admitted that they could not accomplish such a thing were typically dismissed. This discursive tack more frequently ended up qualifying death-prone jurors—those whose personal feelings held that anyone convicted of capital murder should receive the death penalty. They were more likely than life-prone jurors to agree to put their personal feelings aside. Prosecutors relied on the language of objectivity, metaphors of the mind, and allegiance to honesty and the juror oath in order to qualify these death-prone jurors. Judges, too, more often than not, did their own rehabilitating along the same lines.

Additional research on death penalty juries has suggested that once a defendant is found guilty of a capital crime, a preponderance of jurors believe that the law requires them impose a sentence of death (Eisenberg and Wells 1993). Some of the jurors I talked with reiterated this notion, interpreting "following the law" to mean that it necessarily leads to a death sentence after a capital conviction. I spoke with one juror who was particularly critical of the role of jurors in capital sentencing. As he explained, his jury's penalty deliberations had continued for some time and the jurors were beginning to wear down, still trying to do the right thing:

> J: You know that it's, uh, and they were trying to say and *trying to follow the law*. And everything. And most of the people that realized why the jury was there.
>
> R: What do you mean by that?
>
> J: Uh the jury's there to give the prosecutors, the judge, and the state a free ride. Because a man—c- uh, if somebody's convicted of capital murder, I mean they're accused of it, they can confess to it. But *if the state wants to give him the death penalty*, a judge can't do that. *It's got to be the jury.*

This man's jury was trying to follow the law, but their ultimate role, he claimed, was to give the state a "free ride" in sentencing a man to death. Though they did not admit it nearly as explicitly, many jurors in both my research and others' in fact viewed following the law as leading them down the path of death.

But why were death-inclined jurors more easily qualified in this manner? I suggest it is because the consequences of a death-inclined juror putting aside his personal beliefs are not commensurate with those of a juror who doesn't believe in the death penalty doing the same. That is, if a death-inclined juror says, yes, I can put my feelings aside and follow the law, the consequence of going against their personal opinion is that a defendant receives a life sentence. In the converse situation, if a life juror says I will set aside my feelings and follow the law, then the defendant receives a death sentence. People who do not believe in the death penalty are far less likely to put aside their beliefs in the name of the law if that potentially means taking someone's life. The result is that those jurors who are qualifiable tend to be those who believe in death and thus have, from a subjective point of view, a less substantial emotional hurdle to overcome in order to follow the law.

With the contradictory instructions jurors receive and the push and pull they experience from attorneys and judges regarding whether they should or should not allow their emotions to play into their decisions, I am left wondering whether death penalty law can and should acknowledge, explicitly, to jurors that following the law does not necessitate abandoning all emotion; that in fact, the two can beneficially coexist. As anyone who has sat through a death penalty trial can attest, emotion will always play a role in death penalty verdicts, despite jurors' claims that they can set it aside. The question is how jurors can be empowered to harness their emotion in such a way that does justice to justice.

While research on juries, emotion, and legal decision-making suggests that emotion can be instructed away in criminal trials, this chapter has demonstrated that the implementation of such an ideology can have deleterious effects for capital defendants. Attorneys', judges', and jurors' attempts, moreover, to cling to an objective ideal of law, in which emotion does not figure, undermines the constitutional mandate that death penalty cases be decided on personal, moral considerations.

4

Facing Death: Empathy, Emotion, and Embodied Actions in Jurors' Decisions

And it came to me, and I was, I was ready to say that I cou—I was, I started crying. I said, you know, when he took the stand, 'cause he got to testify, and I told everybody I was waiting for a plea. I was waiting for "I'm sorry." I don't know what I was thinking. I was waiting for that, waiting to return that change, that different I was waiting for it in his eyes. I was waiting for it in what he was saying in his voice, in his, in his demeanor. I didn't see none of that. And there is, no I don't, there's, there's I don't see any hope for him.

—FORMER TEXAS CAPITAL JUROR

THE WORDS ABOVE COME FROM a former Texas capital juror, Raul. He was telling me about his jury's initial voting poll during their punishment phase deliberations. When Raul's turn came, he was overwhelmed with emotion. As he expressed his willingness to give death ("I was ready to say that I [could vote for death]"), he turned to the defendant—Travis Gilbert's—testimony. It was not simply the content of his testimony on which Raul remarked, however. Gilbert's demeanor, his voice, his eyes left an impression on Raul, and it is these actions that led him to determine: "I don't see any hope for him." Comments about defendants' behavior beyond their words permeated my interviews with jurors. Despite jurors' reliance on such behavior in their decisions, however, they were confronted with and constructed their own ideologies that deemed nonverbal behavior insignificant and potentially dangerous to jury decision-making.

Visual representations of criminal trials abound in American imaginations, propelled by fictional television shows and movies, as well as the increasingly popular coverage of real trials on Court TV and the like. These depictions often capitalize on the assumption that embodied communicative actions in trials—defendants' facial expressions, the gestures of attorneys and witnesses—are often paramount in jurors' decision-making (Remland 1994). Despite this widely recognized phenomenon, legal scholarship and practice often operate as if these material components of legal decision-making can—and should—be stripped from jurors' judgments (Levenson 2008). All of this in the name of impartiality and justice (e.g., Burnett and Badzinski 2005; Rafter 2006; Searcy, Duck, and Blanck 2004). This chapter destabilizes this view of legal decision-making by querying how a variety of multi-modal, embodied actions within death penalty trials and legal restrictions placed on them may curtail jurors' abilities to empathize with defendants, especially when judging their motives, intentions, and, most significantly, their remorse.

In practice and in academia, law has been firmly established as a profession of words. Lawyers quibble over the precise verbiage to use in closing arguments. Legal theorists recognize that a trial is constructed of multiple, fragmented narratives, none of which adds up to a singular truth (e.g., Brooks and Gewirtz 1998). Critical legal scholarship attributes law's violence—its power over people—to the binding, Austinian force behind its words (Constable 2014; Cover 1986). Less established is the understanding of law as a communicative event, in all that the word communication entails. While linguists, anthropologists, and others have thoroughly examined the multimodal nature of language and meaning (e.g., Ochs 2012; Goodwin 2003; Singer, Radinsky, and Goldman 2008; Hutchins and Palen 1997; Streeck, Goodwin, and LeBaron 2011), moreover, ideologies also remain within these fields that assume a rift between language and embodied experiences and actions, including empathy and emotion. The latter are considered, accordingly, too individualized to be captured through linguistic means. In this perspective, language belies empathy and emotion. Talk lies, in other words (Haviland 1989, 32).

PARALINGUISTIC IDEOLOGIES

Jurors with whom I spoke maintained beliefs that nonverbal communication—which they largely considered distinct from written and verbal forms—should be excluded as bases for their decisions in the jury room. Comments about such "nonlinguistic" actions were nonetheless pervasive in their trial recollections, but jurors often explained them away as irrelevant and even harmful to making legal decisions. Thus jurors' ideologies appear to differ greatly from their actual practices; their beliefs about what they should rely on in making decisions contradicted the actual content of these decisions.

I use the framework of *paralinguistic ideologies*[1] to explore these issues, conceived both as a practical and an analytic concept. *Language ideologies*—a topic of interest in linguistic anthropology since the 1980s—reveal the usually implicit, sometimes explicit, linkages between language users' ideas about language and culture and their actual linguistic practices (e.g., Irvine 1989). Language ideologies are never neutral; they are always linked to particular vested interests, especially in institutional contexts (Schieffelin, Woolard, and Kroskrity 1998). Paralinguistic ideologies in legal contexts are similarly patterned on authoritative discourses about rationality and objectivity (as discussed in the previous chapter); racialized, gendered, and socioeconomically grounded notions of appropriate verbal and nonverbal communication (cf. Gruber 2014; Ramos-Zayas 2011); and hierarchies of legal and lay authority in the courtroom and beyond.

The term *paralinguistic ideologies* is meant to capture ideas people have about nonverbal communication, including its oft-assumed distinction from verbal language, and how these ideas affect how people use and orient toward nonverbal aspects of language.[2] Nonverbal communication

1. I am indebted to Elizabeth Mertz for her insightful suggestion of this term. The term "paralinguistic" was first introduced to refer to elements of language beyond the content of utterances themselves, such as pitch, prosody, and intonation (Trager 1958). It has often been used specifically in reference to emotive qualities of communication (e.g., Poyatos 1993). I use it here to refer to any medium or component of communication beyond the content of utterances, including formal aspects of speech as well as nonverbal behavior. My choice of "paralinguistic" is meant to emphasize the inseparability of these phenomena from what is usually thought of as "language."

2. See also Ramos-Zayas's (2011) concept of "quotidian emotional epistemology," which refers to assumptions about and rules regarding affective behavior and its interpretation.

can include a wide array of actions, such as eye gaze, gesture, facial expression, and body orientation, all of which, in conjunction with spoken talk, help construct meaning in any interaction (e.g., Goodwin 2003; Patterson 1983). In the context of capital trials, I specifically address assumptions jurors and attorneys hold about the meanings and appropriateness of defendants' embodied displays during trial, defendants' and jurors' bodily positioning and orientation in the courtroom, jurors' ideas about the relevance of their own embodied reactions to their decisions, and claims that by adhering to specific legal *words*, jurors can occlude embodied experiences from their decision-making in the name of objectivity. This last paralinguistic ideology is particularly salient in jurors' reflections on their decisions, as it stems from the authority of their written instructions and the talk of judges or attorneys (as evidenced in the previous chapter).

Another paralinguistic ideology common to legal contexts is that certain kinds of communicative phenomena reveal the "truth" about a person's inner state, especially one's motives. In one sense, the structure of Anglo-American legal proceedings assumes that nonverbal actions express intent; if someone kills with a gun, rather than a stick, for instance, the intent was more assuredly to kill. Furthermore, legal processes rely in part on the explicit recognition that words can lie—hearsay is rejected in trials as unreliable testimony. In an interesting twist on this logic, however, the "excited utterance" exception to the hearsay rule assumes that statements made during extreme emotional arousal are likely to be true because "raw emotion" trumps cognitive reason in terms of authentically representing one's inner states (Maroney 2006, 130). In other contexts, law relies heavily on *linguistic* expression as a marker of truth and reliability. Consider the recitation of Miranda rights, for instance, during which persons give themselves over to the law by uttering a few prescribed words. A legal sentence, indeed, is first and foremost a linguistic statement that puts into motion a series of very consequential actions (Austin 1962).

Despite the law's ambiguous treatment of language, embodied actions, and truth, many legal scholars argue vociferously that, in the end, in Haney's words, "the dry and disconnected discourse of legal authorization" limits the "full range of human elements" in a juror's decision (Haney 1997, 1485). As Justice Brennan of the Supreme Court has argued, the language of judging must be expanded to reflect the "subjective, experiential, and emotional" influences of decision-making (Henderson 1988, 123; Nussbaum 1996). Contrarily, Bandes argues that there are dangers in allowing such influences on legal processes without "sufficient structural safeguards," for this would invite prejudice and arbitrariness to prevail (1996, 399). Despite these different attitudes about language and emotion/empathy in legal practice, law ultimately relies on words (Daniel 1997, 350), and thus the nature and implications of legal language—in all its forms—should be subject to scrutiny.

The previous chapter illuminated the ambivalent stance death penalty law takes toward emotion in trial. This chapter's exploration of paralinguistic ideologies within capital trials builds on that discussion, showing that in addition to believing that their instructions direct them not to include *their own* sensory and emotional experiences or *those of other jurors* in their decision-making, jurors rely heavily on *defendants'* embodied displays during trial when making their sentencing decisions. Jurors judge remorse, more specifically, through the presence or lack of expected embodied displays from defendants (cf. Eisenberg, Garvey, and Wells 1998). Underlying these ideas about embodied behavior in criminal trials is the prevailing (culturally specific)[3] belief discussed above that nonverbal behaviors somehow reveal one's authentic feelings (Salekin et al. 1995),[4] while language is a device that allows one to disguise them. As linguistic anthropologists and conversation analysts have demonstrated, however, affect is interactionally achieved; emotion is not simply a "dispassionate [mental] state" (Konradi 1999) to be hidden or revealed, but is built through interaction with others.

Death penalty jurors filter defendants' and others' actions through paralinguistic ideologies they receive from the law as well as those they generate themselves through their experiences within and outside of trials. The analyses below are divided into two main sections, both of which explore the import of bodies and embodied actions in trial to jurors' decisions and to their judgment of defendants as human beings:

1. The positioning and institutional maintenance of bodies—especially defendants'—in the courtroom. This section investigates the salience of eye gaze to jurors' empathic responses to defendants.

2. Jurors' expectations and interpretations of defendants' embodied displays of emotion during trial and their impact on jurors' judgments of defendants' level of remorse.

---

3. Comments about such modes of communication were nonetheless pervasive in their trial recollections, but jurors explained them away as irrelevant and even harmful to making legal decisions.

4. Facial expressions in particular have been argued to reveal one's "true inner feelings" (Salekin et al. 1995; Ekman 1993; Ekman and Friesen 1974).

STUDYING PARALINGUISTIC IDEOLOGIES IN CAPITAL TRIALS: A METHODOLOGICAL CAVEAT

It is important here to point out a methodological irony of my research, not simply for the purpose of self-disclosure, but because it is theoretically revealing. It is not legally permitted to record death penalty jury deliberations, and I was not given permission to video-record trials in Texas. I therefore rely on jurors' postdeliberation reflections to elucidate their embodied experiences during trials and deliberations. The irony is this: I am attempting to understand the role of paralinguistic ideologies in juror decision-making, but the law says that I have to do that by verbal reconstruction alone (cf. Gruber 2014, 8).[5] My data collection and analysis are thus limited by law's own *linguistic* ideology, which asserts that the written record is paramount, and its *paralinguistic* ideology, which deems video-recording trials too dangerous to permit. I can therefore only understand jurors' paralinguistic ideologies through secondary evidence, such as jurors' postverdict trial recollections.

I nonetheless seek to forward a perspective on law and language that moves beyond entrenched dichotomies of language and experience described previously. Embodied actions such as eye gaze and emotional reactions to others present in trials are crucial to how jurors interpret defendants' moral and legal accountability (e.g., Manzo 1996). These practices, however, do not easily fit into the textual schema by which legal professionals define evidence (Levenson 2008). This requires that we view trials as more than a collection of transcripts and

---

5. While certain states are beginning to rely on videotaped trial records in addition to written transcripts, appellate courts are still very reluctant to use video records in their decisions (Owen and Mather 2000).

be more attentive to the extraverbal and interpersonal actions that are also critical parts of legal practices. In contrast to the disembodied, institutional subject who is often cited as the object/subject of law, this chapter investigates this legal subject in practice as a physically present, emotional being, and examines how jurors and other legal actors attempt to deny characteristics that make him a potential object of empathy—in other words, that make him human.

JURORS AND DEMEANOR EVIDENCE

Jurors are generally permitted, via rules of "demeanor evidence," to rely on their "observations of witnesses" in determining the truth of their testimony (*NLRB v. Dinion Cola Co.*, 201 Fed Reporter, 2nd Series 484, 2nd Circuit Ct of Appeals (1951); cited in Conley 1980, 89). The "constant assessment of non-verbal behavioral cues" (Conley 1980, 98) is thus allowed in order for jurors to judge a witness's credibility. There is little legal restraint on what form this assessment takes, so that the jury's role of bringing norms of "everyday human behavior" into the decision-making process may be preserved (Conley 1980). It varies greatly, however, how and to what degree jurors are briefed on such rules.

There exists one major qualification to the admittance of demeanor evidence, however; a fact-finder must only rely on a person's demeanor *while she is giving testimony* and thus must "close its eyes to any human behavior occurring beyond the physical confines of the witness stand" (Conley 1980, 95; *Kovacs v. Szentes*, 33 Atlantic rep., 2nd series 124, Conn Sup Ct (1943)). It has been shown that despite the legal urging to focus solely on events that occur within the context of the witness stand, most jurors use behavior from outside that context to inform their decisions (Rose, Diamond, and Baker 2010; Eisenberg and Wells 1993). Their ideologies, however, often corroborate this ruling's main tenet. Though witness demeanor is not explicitly mentioned in the Texas Rules of Evidence, jurors tended to read their instructions as barring them from considerations of defendants' and other trial participants' demeanor beyond the witness stand. I requote Jed here, whose comments on evidence and emotion were discussed in the previous chapter:

> The charge specif—that we as jurors, every one of us, swore to, on the day of our oath, the charge said that we would *only let evidence guide us.* We would not let supposition, emotion, prejudice, I forget the other term but something like that, okay? So, you must try to put your emotion aside as much as you can and *only go on what is presented as evidence, either from the stand or physical evidence.*

Despite not referring specifically to nonverbal behavior, Jed comments on the tone of the witness's testimony, determining it inappropriate to be considered in his decision. Concordant with the case law cited above, Jed perceives the witness stand as a physical barrier that marks off where evidence begins and ends. Such a barrier is a physical representation of the ideologies expressed by many jurors that sanctioned "evidence" (though rarely defined) can be the only source upon which they rely in their decision-making.

EMPATHY, THE FACE, AND LAW

Actions beyond the witness stand that proved significant to jurors' decisions take many forms. The face-to-face encounter, for instance—a primordial form of interaction—can jar one's deeply seated ideologies through which experience is filtered, and cause one to feel empathy for a person one might not have even considered a person before the encounter. For example, though several jurors I spoke with repeatedly exclaimed (often with a great deal of vigor) that murderers are not people and do not deserve the oxygen they breathe, being forced to be face to face with a convicted capital murderer caused them to unexpectedly empathize with this person and thus begin to consider his humanistic qualities. This process is due in part to how humans come to know others, by "exposure to [others'] bodies moving and acting in ways that we recognize as similar to the ways in which we would act under similar circumstances" (Duranti 2010, 7; see also Rorty 1995). This conceptualization promotes a model of legal reasoning that encompasses affective and empathetic responses to others' bodily actions. Embodied actions, moreover, may actually be more salient in our experiential field than other forms of communicative acts, such as verbal language (Rorty 1995), further justifying a view of legal reasoning that takes this into account.

While being physically present with another, confronted with another's face, can kick-start and intensify empathic and emotional experiences, these experiences are often filtered through particular cultural, institutional sieves (Lynch 2002). For instance, though a juror may feel empathy for a defendant crying on the stand, this empathy is processed alongside notions of why this particular defendant with his particular characteristics is crying and how one should react to it. Jurors' feelings and consequent decisions are thus related not just to the past of the defendant, but to jurors' own complex pasts as well (cf. Throop 2008). For instance, a juror watching a defendant cry on the stand might have long-standing beliefs that those who commit crimes do not deserve pity, and in return might resent the defendant's display of tears. Our bodies at the present moment thus serve as filters through which we perceive/understand the other, as do our cultural, linguistic, and experiential histories.

A question to be investigated is how these conceptions of empathic experience (one primordial, immediate, ignited by the presence of another body; the other, rational, more deliberate, and culturally and linguistically framed) intersect, and if one prevails over the other in certain situations. For instance, Bandes argues that empathy produces counternarratives, in that it allows a juror to imagine himself in the place of another even if it contradicts his own normative narratives (1996, 377). Can looking a defendant in the eye during trial, for instance, allow jurors to empathize with someone they deem evil and thus unworthy of empathy based on their beliefs about actions he has committed?

BODIES IN LAW

The Anglo-American trial system requires a defendant and a jury to be physically present for courtroom proceedings, as "we value a dynamic in which the community literally faces the accused" (Levenson 2008, 53; cf. Mulcahy 2007).[6] The defendant's presence is thus expected, taken for granted even, but rarely examined for its ideological implications. Trials are social encounters, as highlighted previously, and as such involve often repeated face-to-face contact between jurors and defendants. In this sense, the participants in a trial are in constant "dialogue" with one another (Hollan and Throop 2010, 3), though not a dialogue that necessarily involves spoken language. Rather, jurors visually interact with defendants within the "contextual configuration" (Goodwin 2000, 1489) of the trial, which includes the positioning of bodies and material aspects of the environment (cf. Rose, Diamond, and Baker 2010, 311). Jurors are thus not only attuned to the presentation of testimony and evidence taking place in the "official" space of the trial, but are also acutely aware of the "offstage" elements of the courtroom, such as nonofficial participants and official participants' actions that are not formally part of the trial (Rose, Diamond, and Baker 2010). This contextual configuration is institutionally mediated in order to influence ways in which jurors encounter defendants. These mediations have demonstrable effects on jurors' interpretations of defendants' behavior, intentions, and morality.

The spatial arrangement of a courtroom is typically considered a "depoliticized surface," (Mulcahy 2007, 384), organized in regard to practical concerns alone. But it is in fact an integral component of how power relations are structured within our court system (Mulcahy 2007, 385; Foucault 1984; Massey 2005). Anglo-style courts are specifically designed to encourage inclusion and participatory justice, for example, by allowing the press and public to take up a large proportion of courtroom space (Mulcahy 2007, 384). This section examines the implications of body positioning within the built environment of the courtroom, which is designed to allow or disallow jurors certain kinds of sensorial access to defendants.

---

6. Levenson (2008, 55 n. 183) also points out that many jurisdictions will not allow a defendant to waive his right to be physically present for his trial (Fed. R. Crim. Proc. 43(c)(1)(B)) precisely because judging the defendant requires that jurors observe him directly.

Figure 4.1 depicts the arrangement of one courtroom in Texas and is a fairly typical representation of the spatial arrangements of persons in U.S. courtrooms in general. In front of the bar—the physical divider between the gallery (where the public sits) and the court professionals—two tables are placed next to each other. At one sits the prosecution team, usually two or three attorneys, and at the other are the two defense attorneys and the defendant. The defendant usually wears a suit that either his family or his lawyers purchased or borrowed for him. He is not cuffed or restrained in any visible way, a deliberate attempt by the court not to have the defendant's appearance sway the jurors.[7] Because of this specific presentation of the defendant in court, many jurors told me that when they first came into the courtroom for jury selection, they thought the defendant was one of the attorneys. I made the same mistake once as well. How defendants are situated in trials reveals a great deal about how we think of defendants and our criminal legal process in the United States more generally. Defendants in Ukraine, in contrast, are

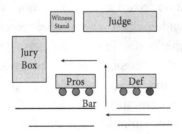

FIGURE 4.1 Arrangement of a typical American courtroom

---

7. The Supreme Court has ruled as to the prejudicial nature of certain visible displays of the defendant. See *Carey v. Musladin* 2006, *Estelle v. Williams* 1976, *Holbrook v. Flynn* 1986.

sometimes held in cages in the courtroom, which indicates a drastically different way of treating the criminally accused.

Implicated within the positioning of bodies in trial is the opportunity for eye contact between defendants and others in the courtroom. In the courtroom diagrammed in figure 4.1, the jurors were processed directly in front of the defendant as they came and went, giving him unimpeded visual access to them. Courtroom procedure required that they enter and leave the courtroom after the defendant was already seated in his place. A number of jurors remarked on the defendant's ready ability to look at them and attempt eye contact as they entered and exited. Many of them actively avoided his gaze, some women going so far as to ask the judge to instruct the defendant not to "stare" at them because it made them uncomfortable. By actively avoiding eye contact with defendants, jurors evaded an encounter at the foundation of empathic engagement (Dadds et al. 2012; Enfield and Levinson 2006; Ochs and Solomon 2010).

This may seem a minor point, but it was a major topic of discussion in my interviews with jurors. An element of the trial not caught on record and certainly not part of the "evidence," the defendant's gaze is nonetheless present and real in jurors' trial experiences. Jurors' comments on defendants' eye contact or lack thereof suggest that they construct their own rules regarding the amount and appropriateness of eye gaze and its communication of one's morality and degree of remorse. Thus any manipulation of this access to the face or jurors' intentional attempts to avoid it serves as a device through which jurors can distance themselves from the defendant's human self (cf. Levinas 1969; 1985).

Attorneys recognize the intensity and vulnerability of face-to-face contact between defendants and jurors, often urging potential jurors during voir dire to look directly at the defendant and state whether they could sentence him to death. This tactic made some venire persons revise their previous statements that they could give the death penalty and disqualify themselves. Take, for example, the following exchange from one Texas capital voir dire between a prosecutor and potential juror:

> P: Now, believing in [the death penalty] and participating in it, that's two different things. I want you to *take a look at Mr. Jefferson* [the defendant] *over here. Can you see him?*
>
> J: *Yes.*
>
> P: What I'd like to know is whether or not you feel like if the evidence was appropriate if you could personally participate in a decision where these questions are answered in such a way that Judge Burdette ordered the death of the defendant. Could you personally participate in that kind of process?
>
> J: It would be hard but—
>
> P: Yes, sir. I understand that . . . do you think that's something you could do?
>
> J: No.
>
> P: You don't think you could participate in that process—personally participate in that process?
>
> J: No, I don't.

This venire person was not able to look at the defendant and admit that he could personally aid in his potential death. Legal critics, beginning at least with the first legal realists, have firmly established the disjuncture between law in the abstract and law in actual life. No other encounter than the face-to-face meeting of defendants and jurors brings this more starkly to light.

DEFENDANTS' PRESENCE AND PERSONHOOD

In addition to how their bodies are positioned in trial, defendants' presence is mediated in other meaningful ways. Their presence in the courtroom is often marked and made explicit when witnesses take the stand, for instance. Witnesses with personal knowledge of a defendant are frequently required to point him out in the courtroom, as the record must reflect that the person being discussed in testimony and the physical being of the defendant are one in the same. The following example is typical of these question/answer sequences and, in this case, was the second time this particular witness had been asked to identify the defendant during the trial:

> P: Okay and *Matthew Leery*, just so we get it straight, is *in the courtroom* still.
> W: Yes.
> P: And he is still *where you pointed* last time, correct?
> W: Yes.
> P: Can you *point to him again* and describe what clothing he is wearing.
> W: He is wearing *khaki jeans and a black long-sleeved shirt.*
> P: Let the record reflect *she's identified the defendant.*

In this case, as in many others, the witness was asked to point out the defendant; many witnesses physically point to his location in the courtroom, after which attorneys often, as here, ask them to cite some identifying characteristic, such as clothing, for the record. This is coupled with an indication of the defendant as a particular type of person: "she's identified the defendant." I spend time on this potentially mundane topic to point out that even in this brief encounter, the defendant's embodied self is mediated in multiple ways: he is identified both as an individual by his proper name, clothing, and physical location in the courtroom, and as a generalized legal type, a defendant.

The next example presents a similar exchange involving the same defendant and a different witness. It illustrates even more clearly the multiple forms of personhood that are indexed when a defendant is identified in the courtroom:

> A: Are you *familiar* with an individual known as *Matthew James Leery*?
> W: Yeah. *I am familiar with Matt.*
> A: Do you see *Matthew James Leery* in the courtroom today?
> W: Right there [pointing to the defendant] in a black shirt.
> A: Let the record reflect he's identified *the defendant, Matthew James Leery.*

Here the attorney identified the defendant by his legal name, a format (first, middle, last) that is typically used to index the formality of a situation (cf. Conley 2008). The attorney framed the question as one of familiarity, which the witness aptly displayed through his shift of reference term from the full proper name to a nickname, Matt. The attorney then reverted to his use of the full proper name, in part for the record, so that it reflected the precise individual being identified, but this also served to shift the identification of the defendant from familiar friend back to legal entity. The witness then physically pointed to the defendant, and he was identified in a third format, as "the defendant." Here, then, the defendant was identified as a person who shares intimate social relationships, indicated by the use of his nickname, as well as a body in the courtroom, and lastly as a legal type.

The polysemy of the defendants' identity in these examples represents the myriad ways jurors encounter defendants. They experience an individual being, alive in the courtroom, but must also deal with his decontextualized identity, presented through testimony and evidence and defined categorically as "defendant" or "accused" or "criminal". In asking how jurors can better fulfill the social roles we wish of them, we should consider how we want them to encounter and evaluate defendants.

DEFENDANTS' OFFSTAGE BEHAVIOR

At the close of Travis Gilbert's trial, Gilbert, who was seated at the defense table surrounded by his attorneys and correction officers, was read his death sentence. During the controversial "witness allocution statement"[8] that followed his sentence—which allows victims' family members to speak directly and unimpeded to defendants—the victim's sister spoke lovingly about the victim's life and character, referring to her as an "angel." Gilbert responded in an explosion of rage, yelling and cursing at the victim's mother, the jury, and the judge. He

8. Article 42.03, Tex. Code Crim. Proc.

was eventually escorted by guards out of the courtroom. I introduce this scene to emphasize its novelty. During my fieldwork, defendants most frequently sat quietly, motionless, with no visible signs of emotion when their death sentences were pronounced to them by the judge. In fact this is how most defendants sat throughout their trials. They did little to draw attention to themselves, in part through efforts by the court system and their attorneys. They wore suits, just as their lawyers did; they were not visibly restrained in any way; and most kept a consistent, flat emotional countenance. In essence, they were nonpresent. Most defendants thus performed the disembodied, rational legal subject quite well. In this example, in contrast, Gilbert embodied the antithetical legal subject. In their post-verdict interviews, a number of jurors expressed relief when describing this episode. To them, it solidified their decision to sentence Gilbert to death. They were relieved they had not made a mistake.

The presence of bodies in trial is crucial to understanding how jurors process evidence and make their decisions because (1) jurors rely a great deal on defendants' emotions when making their sentencing decisions and (2) jurors read defendants' imagined emotions from their embodied displays. Thus in addition to monitoring his eye gaze, jurors attune to the physical presence of the defendant by closely monitoring his interactions with others in the courtroom, especially witnesses (Levenson 2008).

Many capital defendants do not testify in their trials. I heard differing reasons for this; some defense attorneys were afraid that prosecutors would ask defendants to apologize for their crimes and they simply would not comply. Others expressed general fear of the lack of control over their clients during cross-examination. Whatever the reason, because they typically did not hear directly from defendants, jurors paid especially close attention to their actions that were not part of the official presentation of evidence, such as chatting with their attorneys or walking in and out of the courtroom.[9] Jurors have been shown to regard this relatively unobserved behavior—when a defendant or other person assumes they are not the "central object of an audience's attention" (Rose, Diamond, and Baker 2010, 311)—as a more authentic representation of a defendant's self (Rose, Diamond, and Baker 2010; Goffman 1959, 7) than his "on the record" verbal or nonverbal behavior. In contrast to research on civil juries, which finds their dependence on "offstage" behavior of parties to have minimal impact on their decisions (Rose, Diamond, and Baker 2010), defendants' behaviors beyond the boundaries of official evidence were highly salient in Texas capital jurors' reflections on their decisions.

When discussing defendants' behavior off the witness stand, jurors constructed definitions of "normal" emotional displays as markers of a defendant's personhood. Jurors' paralinguistic ideologies thus included a range of emotional displays that jurors expected to see from defendants. Displays that deviated from this range were highly consequential for jurors' sentencing decisions. This process is problematic in legal decision-making, as discussed above, because relying on these expressions of feeling assumes an unproblematic correlation between outer appearance and inner state (Rose, Diamond, and Baker 2010, 1499).

What is interesting about these expected range of emotional displays is that they seem to be applicable, in jurors'

---

9. Eisenberg, Garvey, and Wells (1998, 1619) found, moreover, that capital jurors were more willing to see a defendant as remorseful if he testified.

estimations, to all defendants. In my body of research, at least, the young, white military veteran, the black, middle-aged man with a history of violent behavior, the white, soft-spoken artistic and mentally ill man, and the tattooed, white inmate who had previously attempted suicide were all subject to these same expectations regarding their emotional displays in court. This is one way in which, by becoming a defendant, people lose individual aspects of their identities and are transformed into more or less universalized legal types.

Remorse, specifically, has been proven one of the weightier factors in sentencing decisions of both actual and mock juries (Duncan 2002; Eisenberg, Garvey, and Wells 1998; Garvey 1998; Gerimer and Amsterdam 1989; Sundby 1998; Tsoudis 2002). These decisions often rest, moreover, on the assumption that one can "look" remorseful, and that defendants should display such a countenance. As mentioned in the previous chapter, the Texas jurors with whom I spoke often cited specific embodied actions from defendants, such as facial expressions in reaction to certain testimonies, as primary indicators of defendants' remorse or lack thereof (cf. Savitsky and Sim 1974). And when defendants didn't display such actions, this was marked as highly consequential.[10] A female juror on the James Thatcher case laid out her expectations clearly in regards to his emotional displays:

J: When he cried a couple of times, we did talk about that. You know, when he showed some kind of emotion

---

10. This is in opposition to research findings that suggest defendants' facial expressions of "no emotion" are judged favorably by jurors (Remland 1994, 139).

and it only happened a few times, you know. We did talk about that.

R: And you think that had any impact on (the decision)?

J: On the jur—on the verdict? It probably made us think a little more about, you know, someone who's just going to sit back in his chair the whole time and not react will—you'd probably think wasn't conflicted about it. Or, you know, wasn't remorseful about it. Whereas he seemed like he was, you know, and I think we took that away from the, the couple of times he showed emotion.

This juror deduced that if a defendant showed minimal emotional reaction throughout the trial, he probably felt very little remorse for his crime. Thatcher, on the other hand, cried a few times, thus revealing his supposed inner conflict with and potential remorse for the murders he committed. Though her jury discussed this, it did not prove a significant enough mitigating factor for them to give him a life sentence.

In contrast to Thatcher's, other defendants' behavior was often interpreted as listless, which in the context of a murder trial was jarringly unacceptable for many jurors. Raul, for instance, neared aggression as he recounted Gilbert's lack of emotional expression during trial. He adopted a tone of disbelief bordering on anger during this part of the interview.

> But during that whole trial, he, if you were there, *you too saw it: he had no emotion whatsoever.* He was cold as a snake. Now if someone was sitting in a jury box telling the world what a horrible person I was, I think I would have *at least been a little bit interested in what they were saying. And at least looked at 'em.* I'm not asking him to do any histrion—I wouldn't ask him to do any histrionics or any, you know. But at least *show an*

interest in what's going on. *And he showed none whatsoever.* At any point. He was just *completely cold.* Even when his *kinfolks was sitting right behind him.* Just like they were nothing. *So that played a part in it I'm sure. It did for me anyway.* As a point what he, what, you know, what's his, what would he do? I mean, you know, did he show any *human feeling?*

Raul's judgment of Gilbert's moral character is based on expected embodied actions within the courtroom, especially in relation to others present. Raul characterized Gilbert as having no emotion and being "cold as a snake" because he displayed no apparent interest in the witnesses' testimonies. What would constitute such a display for Raul was left unspecified, but his desire for some sort of embodied display is clear, and the absence of such led him to the conclusion that Gilbert lacked any human feeling. In addition, Raul expected Gilbert to show some connection with his family who were present in the courtroom, and his lack of such illustrates further his lack of caring. Raul used this description of Gilbert's behavior as ultimate justification for his decision to give him the death penalty: "So that played a part in it I'm sure. It did for me anyway."

Jurors also used defendants' offstage behavior as a resource for comprehending actions—such as violent murders—that were otherwise extremely hard to come to terms with. Another juror from Gilbert's case, Nathan, expressed his difficulty trying to process the reality of the crime he and other jurors were confronted with in trial. Gilbert stabbed a woman over one hundred times:

> You don't believe what you're seeing, but, as a, just coming in and saying, this is what happened, all that goes through your mind. Well, what happened? How? Who? Who was, what?

What type, wh—did anybody see? What, what, I mean, you're trying to get all these explanations, make it rationalize, and you can't. And it wasn't until, and that's when, at the beginning you try, and () okay, well, what does he, *did he really do this? They're showing the bloody part, the knife, and then his reaction of just, the nonchalant, you know, nothing.* . . . Okay, *you're not normal. This is not normal.* Because then [after seeing the defendant's reaction] *at that point then you could connect him* with this even though you have the pictures of the fingerprints and then the knife, the scar, and everything.

Nathan reported his expectation that Gilbert would have had some sort of visible reaction to seeing the murder weapon in the courtroom. Gilbert's lack of response left him as confounded as the murder itself did. The affective delivery of these utterances, moreover, replete with stops, hesitations, and repetitions, exhibits that this is something Nathan still struggled with at the present moment of the telling in the interview. And despite the typical evidentiary legal methods of identifying an offender, such as fingerprints and knife patterns embedded in a witness' skin, Nathan could not make sense of the fact that the man sitting in front of him in court actually committed this act—not until he watched Gilbert's reactions to testimony about the murder. When these reactions did not map onto his ideas of how a "normal" human being would act when confronted with such a violent act, he accepted that this "not normal" being in front of him could have done such a thing.

Noticings about the defendant's embodied actions also figured into jurors' assessments of defendants' personhood. As seen above, being human carries with it certain expectations, albeit culturally constructed, about how to interact with others in a courtroom context and, specifically, what displays of emotion are anticipated. In the following excerpt, a juror commented on the defendant, Larry Sampson, laughing along with others in the courtroom:

R: I'm curious, like what impressions you had of the defendant. Throughout the trial or after it, or—

J: *He just seemed to have no expression.* Except there at the end, when, I think it's [the prosecutor] was, I can't remember what he said or whatever, I'm sure I wrote it down in my notes. . . . It's like *I saw him smirk* one time. Yeah. And the day that [the judge] said, okay, we're gonna come back after Christmas, when he meant Thanksgiving, and *we all laughed. And he* [the defendant] *laughed. I thought, oh, he laughed!* Hhhh cause you couldn't help but watch him.

This juror first expressed a fairly common observation about defendants, that Sampson had "no expression" during the trial. She then commented about her surprise at his laughing along with the others in the courtroom, first delineating him from the others through the use of "we all" versus "he." Laughing along with others is a common, human experience, and to be surprised at such an action suggests that the juror assumed the defendant to be something less than a social being. While her reaction could be initially interpreted as speaking to the institutional constraints on actors in the formal setting of a courtroom, in which laughter may be considered inappropriate, she expressed no surprise that other legal actors, such as the judge, were laughing in this context. It is specifically laughter from the defendant that she found notable; it does not fit into the range of expected emotional behavior from someone accused of a capital crime.

Jurors recognized that the defendant's body, especially his face, was a source for them to judge his emotions, which they cited as important when making decisions about his life. As an access point to an other, Levinas argues, the face is vulnerable. It is "exposed, menaced, as if inviting us to an act of violence" (1985, 85–86). Part of this violence rests, I submit, in one's belief that a face reveals something true about another human being. When jurors faced capital defendants, many expected to see emotion, specifically remorse. But this was not often what they saw. Defendants' expressionless faces were read as revealing their lack of normal human emotions and thus their lack of humanity. But just as facing another can invoke a denial of one's humanity, it can also incite empathy.

This tendency to read one's face as an authentic and complete representation of an other is both culturally specific (Hollan and Throop 2011) and problematic in the context of legal trials. One of the female jurors on Thatcher's trial astutely related the complexities of confronting a defendant's face:

R: So as the trial went on, um, did your impressions of the defendant change at all?

J: Yes. Sure. Like um, mostly when the defense started talking about, you know, that, uh, how he was—well you know, I take that back. Whenever they started introducing the things that he did as from the prosecution, it kind of made it look like, you know, look different to me after they started talking about all the different things that he did. You know. And then again when it was first, when we first found out that he was in the army and that he was in—had those troubles over there, it makes, develops a whole story. I'm sure that happens all the time, right? *You see a face, you have none of the story. You just know these two things about him.*

She recognized that her initial impressions based on her encounter with Thatcher in the courtroom did not tell his whole story. These impressions changed when his story was filled in with evidence from both sides. So while the face may indeed incite empathy, which defense attorneys would encourage in order to help save their clients' lives, face-to-face encounters can also cause jurors to judge a defendant on brief and limited displays of his character.

According to another juror, being face to face with the defendant indeed inspired empathy with him. This juror wrestled with her experience observing Thatcher throughout the trial, wondering even at the time of the interview what kind of person he was. The juror highlighted his nonverbal displays in parsing her understanding of him. This excerpt reveals her empathic response to her face-to-face encounters with him, as well as the vulnerability they incited, as his personhood was put into question.

> But he was um, *he handled himself um, he was very reserved* in through the whole process. Um, so it was um you—in the beginning *you couldn't read anything from him at all, you know. And they probably wanted it that way.* . . . And I couldn't tell anything and I a couple of times I cau—I tried to catch my—I tried to, to not be so obvious and try to study him and try to say, okay, well what, you know, *he's a person.* You know, what, *what's going on in his mind right now?* You know he's been here all day long. This is only the third, you know, first or second session, you know. *He's been here all day long and what's going on with him?*

Her initial assessment was one of lack of emotion—Thatcher was "reserved" and unreadable. But she then explicitly recognized their commonality—he's a person—and took an empathic stance, wondering how he was handling the trial that she also had to endure. The juror additionally acknowledged a limitation to reading the defendant's face. The reading may not reveal an inner truth, she recognized, but instead that the defendant was coached by his attorneys to appear reserved. It is telling, however, that the juror needed to remind herself that the defendant is a "person" at all. This relates to arguments, such as Haney's, that being a defendant in a murder trial starts the defendant out at the level of "other"—other than human, we might surmise.

Many jurors desired not only emotional displays from defendants, but also some sort of contact with them. While some jurors, as I mentioned before, avoided face-to-face contact with defendants, Raul explained that he wanted Gilbert to testify in his case so he could hear his words and connect with him in some way:

> You know, I want to but, I want to hear what he's going to say, and I want to see what, how, he's going to say it. You know, it's like everything was like, that was a pivotal moment for me. . . . And he was a—*he couldn't even look at us.* He couldn't, I mean, and it was like this isn't for real. This is—it's nothing.

In this account, Gilbert's lack of emotional display was a "pivotal moment" in Raul's decision-making. He highlighted his desire to see Gilbert's embodied behavior during his testimony. More specifically, he desired some sort of embodied connection between Gilbert and the jury. What he got instead, to his shock, was a lack of what Raul believed to be even the remotest sign of empathy from Gilbert: eye contact.

This lead to Raul's ultimate judgment that Gilbert lacked remorse for his crime.

Like Raul, many jurors were also intensely interested in hearing a defendant's voice during trial, though such voices are highly mediated by legal rules (Matoesian 2008a), just as defendants' bodily actions are. Defendants are not permitted to address the judge or jury directly unless they are put on the witness stand, which is fairly rare in capital trials. Their voices are thus filtered throughout the entire trial by their attorneys. Because of this, points at which a defendant's voice does come through, such as in his rare testimony, audiotaped phone calls or confessions, or letters he wrote, are coveted by jurors when making their decisions. In this next interview excerpt, a juror told me the importance of reading a letter a defendant, Sampson, wrote to his brother after the crime, and whether it supported the defense's theory that Sampson was suicidal:

> His *own* letter that bragged upon his outlaw status. That wanted his brother to be sure and save all of his newspaper clippings. That bragged upon dying an outlaw's death. That castigated his brother for not sending him money so he could buy stuff at the commissary. *These are not the words and actions* of a person who's contemplating suicide.

This juror highlighted the fact that this letter was Sampson's "own" and thus a valuable, authentic form of his voice (cf. Bauman and Briggs 2003; D'hondt 2009; Goffman 1981; Gumperz 1983). The letter was offered as a resource for understanding the nature of and motivations behind his actions: wanting, bragging, and castigating. One's voice, one's whole body, is a marker of one's humanity, and thus how it is constrained and recontextualized in the trial setting is crucial for jurors' interpretations and ability to judge one's actions (cf. Matoesian 2008a).

In a poignant reflection on one defendant who *did* testify on his own behalf, Gilbert, we hear from the following juror his belief that hearing directly from a defendant accurately reveals his inner state. The juror discussed his surprise at the prosecutor's (Mr. Blanke's) tactic when cross-examining Gilbert.

> I thought it was so awesome of Mr. Blanke when he said, this is your chance. Go ahead. Tell, tell the jury why they shouldn't vote for you to be killed. Go ahead. This is your chance, your opportunity. And I thought it was so amazing, because we were all looking forward to, what is he going to say? What is Mr. Blanke, this, you know, wonderful attorney, going to go and wha—how is he going to tear him up? And instead of him doing anything, *he just totally left the leash off and said okay, go on. Go for it.* And that was so awesome he did because you saw, *we saw, the true person.* . . . And then it was like it was, like, oh. Like a disappointment. And then we *hear him talk*, and then it was, like, oh, a disgust. Like, this is terrible. You're going to expect us to believe what you're saying? He could not, he couldn't bring it to himself. To say sorry. He couldn't.

Because of the relative lack of mediation of Gilbert's voice—the prosecutor gave him free reign in a sense to talk on the stand—this juror felt he was privy to the "true person." What came out of Gilbert's refusal to apologize when given this free reign was supposed proof of his lack of remorse, which, for this juror, was met with disgust.

In addition to defendants' behavior, I also found jurors to be astutely observant of *witnesses'* embodied encounters with and reactions to defendants. Gilbert, for instance, had a particularly aggressive personality, which he did not always conceal well despite his attorneys' urgings. During the penalty phase testimony, the prosecution called one of Gilbert's previous girlfriends to the stand. She had asked ahead of time to be escorted up to the stand by a guard (which is not common), who placed his body between her and the defendant when he walked her up. When I asked a juror from this trial what testimony he found significant in the punishment phase, he replied with a reference to this witness:

> The girlfriends' testimonies. Especially the one that was, you know, was kidnapped and taken out. I mean, I feel terrible for her. After all these years still is a vivid memory to her and a terror. I'm not sure whether *the security guard stood up between them* if that was not posturing on the part of the prosecution or not, but I think she still appreciated it. I mean, I think she's going to sleep a little better.

The witness's fear of being physically present with the defendant elicited sympathy from this juror. He recognized that placing the witness in Gilbert's proximity evoked the terror she felt when he kidnapped her in the past. The juror perceptively recognized, however, that these embodied interactions can be manipulated by attorneys in order to stir jurors' emotions. Jurors and attorneys alike acknowledge the rich source these embodied actions can be for influencing jurors' decisions.

Another juror in the same trial reflected on his own intense emotional reaction to seeing a victim who survived Gilbert's attack (this victim's mother did not), a nine-year-old boy, confront his attacker in the courtroom.

> And you know here I was, you know, here I was crying, thinking, you know, man, this *poor, poor boy* is coming in to the witness stand *in front of the person who just* did this to him and did this to, did this to his mother. You know, what, what could

be going on in his mind right now. It's like, you know, and he did such a great job.

The juror was shocked at how well the boy handled such an emotionally rife and potentially traumatizing encounter, again, sharing sympathetic feelings with the witness who was forced to be physically proximal to the defendant. And though the crime occurred four years prior to the trial, this juror spoke of the murder as though it had just happened ("just did this to him"). Similar to the above example, in which being in front of the defendant invoked in the present situation the witness's feelings of terror that she experienced when attacked by him in the past, this juror expressed the sense of temporal proximity and, in turn, emotional intensity that is induced when one is in the physical presence of another.

My discussions with capital jurors revealed, in contrast to previous research on jurors' ideas about remorse (Eisenberg et al. 1998), that the viciousness of the crime did not correlate to any demonstrable degree with jurors' willingness to read remorse from defendants. What seemed more salient were jurors' own ideas of how normal persons would act and react when on trial for vicious crimes they committed. Defendants' behavior that departed from these expectations led jurors to conclude that defendants lacked remorse and thus, in most cases, deserved to be sentenced to death.

SEEING FACES, FEELING BODIES IN CAPITAL TRIALS

Empathy is frequently cited as a salient factor in criminal sentencing and is typically discussed as both enhanced and restricted by social identity factors such as race and socio-economic status (e.g., Haney 2003). This chapter has endeavored to show that physical proximity and direct interaction with another should also be considered incitements to empathy in criminal trials (Henderson 1987, 1586).[11] Jurors' empathic experiences are facilitated by being physically present with another's body, and these experiences shape jurors' empathy with, understandings of, and judgments of defendants. Husserl's (1989;1969) notion of intersubjectivity captures the importance of bodies in our understandings of others:

> The Body [is] the bearer of the zero point of orientation, the bearer of the here and the now, out of which the pure Ego intuits space and the whole world of the senses. Thus each thing that appears has eo ipso an orienting relation to the Body, and this refers not only to what actually appears but to each thing that is supposed to be able to appear. (Husserl 1989[1913], 61)

Husserl identifies not just the body of the other, but that of the self as central to our interpretations of the world around us (including other bodies). Through bodies, we come to understandings that are not propositional and rational in content but are, rather, "automatic and often reflex-like" (Gallese 2003, 520). Jurors are not disembodied finders of fact— floating minds in the jury room—as the legal system often constructs them, but experience embodied encounters with others in the courtroom that are often incredibly salient to how they interpret defendants' actions and motives. In that

---

11. Though intersubjective and empathic experience is of course possible without the physical presence of an other (Duranti 2010, 10; Heidegger 1996; Husserl 1989[1913]).

the physical copresence of bodies is the basis for empathic experience, jurors do not necessarily have to share common experiences with defendants in order to understand their actions, as some legal scholars have argued (Gobert 1988, 278; see also Lutz and White's analysis of Bourdieu's "positioned subject" [1986], 415).

Jurors' reflections explored above reveal common patterns among their understandings of their decision-making roles. First, they illustrate a stance toward defendants' bodies as intentional, controlled objects, and their actions as therefore willfully connected to and accurately representative of their internal states. Embodied behavior, however, also includes preconscious activity and as such is problematic when viewed merely as a vehicle of communication (Streeck 2003). Jurors' assumptions that all (especially offstage) embodied actions of defendants reveal directly their guilt, remorse, or other emotional state is thus problematic.

These examples also demonstrate the intractability of jurors' notions of legal objectivity and the problems entailed in instructing jurors on how to deal with embodied experiences—both theirs and others'—in their decisions. What is a juror to do with his reactions to a defendant's deadpan face in trial? What channels of reason and facticity can such reactions be filtered through in order to make a legal judgment? What about the jurors' own emotional reaction to a bloody knife in the courtroom and to his exposure to a violent crime?

Emotional displays from witnesses and others *besides the defendant*—including jurors themselves—were often considered immaterial and even inappropriate to consider when making their decisions, as illustrated in Jed's response. *Defendants'* embodied actions, however, were monitored closely by jurors and carefully considered during their deliberations. Specifically, the *absence* of defendants' emotional displays was read by jurors as proof of their culpability and lack of remorse for criminal acts. As attorneys and others are aware, however, the intentions behind such lack of emotional displays are varied and may be due to attorney coaching, or to defendants' common ethos that displaying emotion is not a proper action in which a man should indulge.

Jurors nonetheless used ideologies of the primacy of legal *words*—as seen with Jed—to deny experiences of empathy with defendants and thus sentence them to death. While I can opine on the theoretical violence that's exacted on defendants through the domination of these ideologies, their practical implications are just as pervasive and potentially more alterable. I have had countless conversations with attorneys and judges about these issues throughout my time working on death penalty trials. During the first trial I observed, for instance, I suggested to the defense attorneys that they not include a so-called sympathy clause in the jurors' sentencing instructions, which required them not to rely on sympathy in their decisions. My opinion was based on an intuition, later confirmed, that jurors would use such verbiage to deny empathy with the defendant and sentence him to death. The attorneys wanted to include the clause to instruct jurors not to rely on their reactions to victims' and their families' emotions in making their decisions. When jurors are instructed to refrain from allowing feelings into their decisions in any context, however, they tend to generalize this to mean that only recordable aspects of testimony, that is recordable in morphological form, are relevant to their decisions. This situation reveals an irony in law in its promotion of emotional testimony and simultaneous instruction to jurors not to use it.

The complexities of these issues are innumerable, so I will focus on one last wrinkle within them to close. The defendant's fate in part lies, as Levinas would predict, both in the presence and in the vulnerability of his face to the jurors. The attorneys' directives for potential jurors to look the defendant in the eye during voir dire are consequential and prescient. When faced with this phenomenological shift, many jurors reflected that their thoughts about the death penalty and criminal justice had changed since they filled out the juror questionnaire only weeks or, for some, hours before. This face-to-face encounter, being copresent with the defendant and looking him in the eyes, often led venire persons to disregard legal rhetoric about being objective and rational, and simply admit that they could not be good jurors in this situation. Those that did accept the task often relied on the legal authority of evidence and rationality to bar emotion from their decisions. Some jurors in fact used this logic to convince others holding out for life to change their mind.

In addition, part of the reasoning behind the law's and jurors' attempts to curtail empathic encounters is to make the process of sentencing someone to death more palatable to the jurors. Jurors themselves recognized, however, that when engaged face to face with another person, no matter how many institutional regulations are in place to make the decision easier, denying someone their life is no easy task. As one juror acknowledged,

> That's the hardest thing I've ever had to do, to look at a man and, you know, know that I'm saying, you know, I don't think you should live.

Thus, this basic source for empathic understanding, the meeting of eyes, caused unease for this juror to give the death penalty. Despite this unease, however, he voted for death. In the examples given above, jurors pointed to physical or emotional cues that were conspicuously absent to them in their interactions with or experiences of the defendant to justify their decisions to sentence him to death. The legal institution provides jurors with the language and attitudes that enable them to restrain their empathy toward another human being, in order that they may live with the decision that someone else will die.

5

Linguistic Distance and the Dehumanization of Capital Defendants

Soldiers "were able to bring themselves to kill these civilians primarily through application of the mental leverage provided to them by the distance factor. Intellectually, they knew what they were doing. Emotionally, the distance involved permitted them to deny it."

—GROSSMAN *2009, 101–102*

SCHOLARS AND LEGAL PRACTITIONERS CONTINUALLY struggle with the central question of this book: how can a juror sentence another human being to die? A prevailing answer suggests that jurors find ways to distance themselves from defendants (Haney 2004; Garvey 2000), often promoted by differences such as race and socioeconomic dissimilarity (Lynch and Haney 2011). This distance forges an "empathic divide" between jurors and defendants, ultimately allowing jurors the moral leeway to commit another person to death (Haney 2004).

The previous chapter explored ways in which jurors mediate *physical* distance in face-to-face encounters with defendants. This chapter looks beyond the negotiation of physical distance, demonstrating how empathy with defendants can be "suppressed, obstructed and misled" (Hatab 2002, 255) through written and verbal language. As attorneys are already well aware, calling a defendant "that guy" in a trial has a much different impact on a jury than referring to him as "Steven" or "Mr. Black." But why? How can such a subtle difference in word choice affect how jurors and others perceive or feel about a defendant?

By analyzing how attorneys, witnesses, and jurors talk about defendants—both in trial and in postverdict interviews—the following analyses address this very question. I argue that speakers can mark degrees of distance between themselves and defendants by referring to them through particular forms of what linguists call *deixis*. Deictics are words (or gestures) that require contextual information—the persons involved in a conversation and its spatial and temporal positioning—in order to make sense (see Buhler 1982). For instance, using the word "you" in talk requires that there is a second person, besides the speaker, present in the conversation who is being directly spoken to. Lack of knowledge of who exactly is being addressed would render "you" meaningless.

Speakers always have a choice when referring to a person; they can use a first name, a pronoun such as "she," a description such as "the lady with the red skirt," and so on. Given this pool of choices, referring to someone in a particular way tells listeners something about the speaker's stance toward the person referred to (Haviland 2007;

Schegloff 1996) and in the context of capital trials, can be read as a commentary on a referenced person, such as a defendant. Deictic reference forms, including constructions such as "that guy" and "this defendant," for instance, have been shown to convey emotional distance, lack of empathy, and negative affect towards defendants (Duranti 1984, 302–303; see also Haviland 2007, 250). Because of their ability to encode distance, deictic reference forms allow jurors to keep defendants emotionally at bay, therefore facilitating "psychological barriers" (Haney 1997, 1454) necessary to sentence them to death. These forms also depersonalize defendants, as their lack of specificity obscures the actual person being referred to (cf. Carrithers 2008). In establishing distance from and discouraging the individual identification of defendants, deictic reference forms enable jurors to dehumanize defendants, thereby legitimizing sentences to end their lives.

Empathy[1] and deixis both entail relationships within space, whether physical or metaphorical. Anthropologist Jason Throop, for instance, suggests that empathy relies on the "visceral and emotional *emplacement* of our being in [various] contexts" (2010, 771, emphasis added). In similar fashion, William Hanks, a linguistic anthropologist who has written extensively on the sociocultural meanings of deixis, argues that deictic forms reveal "how the subject *places himself or herself in the physical world*" (1990, 6, emphasis added). My analysis of empathy and deixis within talk about capital defendants derives from the concept of spatial relations upon which both concepts rely.

---

1. Refer back to chapter three for a discussion of empathy and how it is defined in this book.

PROXIMITY AND EMPATHY

The relationship between empathy and proximity has long been an area of study, especially in the field of psychology. In their examination of encounters between therapists and patients, for instance, psychologists Haase and Tepper (1972) outline the nonverbal actions that increase a sense of empathy with a patient, such as eye contact, leaning one's torso toward the patient, and otherwise closing the physical distance between patient and therapist. These embodied actions are understood to increase the sense of physical proximity to a patient and are thus judged as heightening the level of empathy the patient feels from the therapist. In Milgram's (1974) influential, though problematic, study,[2] subjects were told they were administering electric shocks to unknown "victims." The subject was less likely to administer the shock if the victim's body was somehow made more immediate to the subject, either through hearing their voice or seeing their body in an adjoining room. This implied that empathy was increased with increased proximity to the victim, thus making it more difficult for subjects to inflict what they thought was physical harm.

In his account of soldiers killing in modern warfare, Grossman (2009) outlines multiple dimensions of distance that can affect one's ability to kill another human being. Sociocultural elements such as racial and ethnic distance, beliefs in moral superiority, and the social perception of a particular group as less than human can diminish empathy with another just as physical distance does. In regards to the death penalty, Garvey (2000) similarly finds that racial divides

2. Milgram's study has been widely critiqued on ethical and methodological grounds. A discussion of contemporary applications of his research can be found in Blass, ed., 2000, *Obedience to Authority: Current Perspectives on the Milgram Paradigm*, Lawrence Erlbaum.

make it less likely that jurors will empathize with capital defendants. By broadening the notion of proximity to include emotional, experiential, and psychic planes, we open up the field of language to reveal the experiential relations it entails and facilitates.

As revealed through these studies, the capacity for empathy relies at least in part on our physical access and proximity to others. This capacity is often considered to provide the foundation for concern for and understanding of others (cf. Heidegger on "care" [1962] 1996). Adam Smith's account of sympathy,[3] for example, rests importantly on the concept of proximity, for "physical proximity begets familiarity, which makes affection stronger, understanding more accurate, sympathy likelier, and other-concern more natural and appropriate" (Forman-Barzilai 2005, 190, Smith [1759] 1982). Smith's account derives in part from Hume's treatise on sympathy in his *Enquiry Concerning the Principles of Morals*: "Sympathy, we shall allow, is much fainter than our concern for ourselves, and sympathy with persons remote from us, much fainter than that with persons near and contiguous" ([1751] 1983, 99). According to these accounts, sympathy, or concern for others, is thus based in our relative distance from those others.

3. Hume and Smith define sympathy as the intersubjective production of morality. It lacks the affective valence that the contemporary meaning of sympathy evokes and thus more closely resembles current notions of empathy. It is worth, however, taking a brief moment to comment on the difference between the two (see Wispe 1986 for the history of both terms), as they are commonly and, many argue, inappropriately, used interchangeably. While empathy (*Einfuhlung*) tends to refer to a projection of the self into a perceived object (Lipps 1903) or being, which simultaneously entails a separation between self and other (Husserl 1989, 1969; Stein1989), sympathy describes ways in which we are affected by and in turn strive to understand or know the feelings of others (Scheler 1954). The notion of sympathy thus propelled later theories of the innate capacities for humans to respond to the emotions of other humans (Wispe 1991, 1986; McDougall 1908; Darwin 1871). *Einfuhlung* does not necessarily include this affective component.

EMPATHY, PROXIMITY, AND LANGUAGE

Just as physical distance alters empathic experiences with others, linguistic relations of distance also shape our experiences of empathy. This is achieved through the relative positioning among people and things that language facilitates. Linguistic deixis is an exemplary phenomenon by which to understand this negotiation of linguistic distance. Most basically, a deictic term situates a given referent within a spatial universe that is related specifically to the context of talk (e.g., Hanks 1990; see also Lyons 1977; Fillmore 1982). In other words, deictic terms such as *this* or *that, here* or *there* place an object close to or far away from the speaker and others involved in a conversation. When a speaker points to and identifies "that pen," for instance, they are usually referring to a pen positioned relatively far from them. Deictic forms are categorized according to whether they denote a proximal or distal positioning of the speaker to the object referred to (or something along a proximal-distal continuum), *that* encoding more distance than its alternative, *this*.

Linguists have expanded deictic relationships of *spatial* proximity to include other dimensions, such as *social* and *affective* distance (Ostman 1995). These deictic forms, referred to as "emotional" (Lakoff 1974; Ostman 1995) or "empathetic" (Lyons 1977) deixis,[4] display affective relationships among speakers and those they refer to. A particular deictic term can thus display the level of empathy or involvement a speaker has

---

4. Levinson (1983) argues these empathetic uses of deictic forms are in fact not examples of deixis, but are alternative uses of the same pronouns.

with a referent (Duranti 1984; Ostman 1995; Cornish 2001). For example, Duranti (1984) argues that in Italian conversation, the demonstratives *questo/a* (this) and *quello/a* (that), when used instead of personal pronouns, display lack of empathy or negative affect toward the person being referred to. Thus while deictic terms can position things within the physical world in which a conversation takes place, they can also position a person within the moral world created through talk. Deixis thus mediates our relationships with entities and persons of which we speak by positioning these beings within a "lived space," which our "interests, cares, and attention define" (Ochs and Capps 1995, 63, cf. Heidegger 1996).

DEIXIS AND REFERENCE TO DEFENDANTS

While reading and re-reading my piles of transcripts from trials and juror interviews, I was struck by something. Defendants, I noticed, were consistently being referred to in a particular way, as "that guy" or "that defendant." Indeed, my data are replete with references to defendants, and a large portion of them are accomplished through the form *demonstrative adjective + noun*. Upon realizing this, I scoured capital jury interviews from other books written about death penalty jurors and found the same patterns there as well. Following conversation analyst Manny Schegloff's indispensable adage, *Why that now?* my task in analyzing these reference forms was to question why "that man," for instance, was used to indicate the defendant in a particular moment of talk by a particular person and in what contexts this construction was used over and over again.

The examples analyzed in this chapter are drawn from a variety of cases and a variety of speakers. In attempting to answer *Why that now?* I had to rule out some preliminary explanations for why a demonstrative reference form might be used in each context of talk. Conversation analysts have demonstrated that people prefer to reference people with "minimal" forms, usually a proper name or personal pronoun (e.g., "he" or "she") (Sacks and Schegloff 1979; see also Stivers 2007). For instance, the form "Steve" is generally preferred over "the man with the beard," as it uses fewer words. This maxim can be violated when a person is introduced for the first time into a conversation (Schegloff 2007a; 1996; Sacks and Schegloff 1979; see also Gundel, Hedberg, and Zacharski 1993) or when the hearer is not likely to recognize the referent (Sacks and Schegloff 1979). Demonstrative noun phrases, such as "this man," can be used in this context—to bring a new, unidentified referent into focus (Hanks 2005; Schegloff 1996; Schiffrin 1994; Strauss 2002, Levinson 1983; Ehlich 1982; Fillmore 1982). I have thus eliminated from my data sample those cases in which the defendant is first introduced; each instance of reference analyzed was one in which all parties to the conversation (either legal actors in a trial or a juror and I in an interview) already knew quite well who the defendant was. I could therefore not explain the demonstrative reference forms I found in this way.

A second potential explanation is that these forms were examples of "pure deixis" (Buhler 1982), which places an object or person in the spatial context of talk. For example, the utterance "Put it on *that* table," often accompanied by a pointing gesture to a particular table, helps delineate for listeners which table the speaker is singling out. The examples analyzed below, however, are not of this sort either. In order to make sure of this, I eliminated from my corpus of demonstrative reference forms all that could potentially have been of this kind, where a person might have been using "this" or "that" to refer spatially to the defendant in the courtroom. Neither of these explanatory tacks, then, was the right one. I was still left to account for why the *demonstrative adjective + noun* format was being used so often to refer to defendants.

The analyses below reveal my findings: this reference format is frequently used in contexts of linguistic dehumanization, in which jurors, attorneys, and witnesses place distance between themselves and the defendants. These demonstrative reference forms thus do more than just refer to a given person; they *place* him in a particular position via the members of a conversation—not merely in a spatial world, but also in an emotional and moral one. These forms minimize the defendant's identity as a living, individual person, thereby disabling empathy and dehumanizing him. Such actions, produced here through linguistic forms, facilitate and justify the eventual act of killing another human being.

PERSON REFERENCE AND PERSONHOOD

Another part of asking *Why that now?* is considering what possibly could have been said in place of the phenomenon under study. In terms of person reference, one can imagine an almost endless range of alternatives for referencing a person. In a given day, for instance, my mother may refer to me through a variety of names and labels: *Robin* when she's talking to my father, *my daughter* when speaking to the grocery clerk, *Robin Conley* when ordering me a plane ticket, and *Sweetie* when talking to me. The form used, as you can see in these examples, depends both on the context of talk (e.g., is she talking to a stranger or someone who knows both me and her?) and how in particular she wishes to portray me in a given context. Crucial to identifying what is being done by using a particular reference form is thus the relationship (or lack thereof) of the speaker to the referent and any potential audience (Haviland 2007).

Relying on this logic, I posit that third-person reference terms lie on a continuum of intimacy and closeness toward the referent, depicted in figure 5.1 (cf. Gundel, Hedberg, and Zacharski 1993). Indeterminate noun phrases, such as "a man," lie toward the end of generality and lack of definitive, intimate knowledge of the referent. Demonstrative reference forms are also found toward this end of the continuum, with "that" conveying more relative distance than "this," but both depicting more distance than, for instance, proper names (cf. Stivers 2007).[5] However, they denote a higher degree of determinacy than indirect descriptions such as "a man." On the other endpoint lie terms such as "Billy," which

---

5. This position is slightly counter to prevailing theories on demonstrative reference in two ways: First, many claim that the demonstrative *this*, not *that*, is used to draw the referent into the cognitive-discourse sphere of the speaker and/or interlocutor (e.g., Cornish 2001, 312; Levinson 1983, 81). I claim, in contrast, that *that* can accomplish the same action, but it does so in an evocation of a relationship of distance (i.e., it brings the relationship of distance between speaker/interlocutor and referent into focus). Second, while the demonstrative *this* is often considered to show identification or emotional closeness with the referent (e.g., Cornish 2001, 305; Levinson 1983, 81), my data reveals that *this*, just as *that*, can be used to indicate a relationship of distance between the speaker/interlocutor and referent. *That*, however, is never used to depict a relationship of closeness, while *this* may be in some cases. My analyses thus demonstrate that the use of the demonstrative itself is an indication of distance, with the difference between *this* and *that* being a secondary consideration.

Intimacy with, knowledge of the referent

First name	Personal Pronoun	Demonstrative pronoun + noun	Demonstrative pronoun + noun	Definite article + noun	Indefinite article + noun
Billy	He	This man	That man	The man	A man

Lack of specificity regarding referent

Distance between speaker and referent

FIGURE 5.1 Scale of person reference and intimacy

convey a specific kind of intimate knowledge of the referent (cf. Carrithers 2008). As evidence of the ability of reference terms to convey certain degrees of intimacy, take, for example, many tribal peoples, for whom sharing one's first name amounts to sharing one's essence (Stivers, Enfield, and Levinson 2007, 6).

In her haunting account of interviewing former apartheid death squad member Eugene de Kocke, psychologist Gobodo-Madikizela (2003) argues for a similar categorization of reference forms, with first names encoding the highest degree of intimacy. She was heavily conflicted when she found herself empathizing with de Kocke, a killer whom many in postapartheid South Africa consider the epitome of evil. One practice (which did not come easily to her) that enabled this empathy, she reveals, was beginning to refer to de Kocke by his first name; "his first name—that was the *real* him" (Gobodo-Madikizela 2003, 121). Calling him *Eugene* allowed her to establish a necessary stance of engagement with a perpetrator of unthinkable violence. Allowing this engagement, she argues, ensures that perpetrators of violence do not get let off the hook too easily by simply ostracizing them from the human community, but, rather, requires society to confront the evil acts committed and the people who committed them, along with the ideological and political backdrops against which these acts are carried out. Perhaps in criminal trials, defendants should be consistently referred to by their first names in order to ensure that the person, not a mere category, is on trial.

Embedded within this particular continuum of intimacy are multiple other characteristics of person reference. For instance, found somewhere in the middle are reference terms such as "the policeman" that identify people according to a social role or category in which they may be placed (Stivers, Enfield, and Levinson 2007, 2). Descriptions such as these may be more or less specific (Carrithers 2008) and necessarily pick out certain elements of a person's identity at the exclusion of others (Stivers, Enfield, and Levinson 2007, 2). Referring to someone in a legal context as "the defendant" or "an offender," for instance, identifies that person according to a particular legal category and thereby associates him with typical characteristics of people in that category (Schegloff 2007a, 2007b; see also Conley 2008).[6] This form of reference is in fact typical in legal settings, which can be explained in part because in most trials it is not the individual qua individual who is on trial, but his actions, and whether they can be fit into an appropriate legal category.

Thus when a defendant is referred to as "a criminal" rather than as "Bobby" in trial, a number of things are conveyed:

---

6. In a recent bill introduced to the Georgia legislature, a republican representative has requested that state law mandate that rape victims be referred to as "accusers" in all legal proceedings prior to conviction. There has been massive criticism of the bill, which reveals the serious implications that reference to people as certain kinds of legal actors can have.

(1) Bobby's being someone who fits the criteria of "a criminal" and is like others who occupy that category and (2) a lack of intimacy with Bobby's actual person, eschewing a portrayal of his individual personhood for an identification of a type to which his "like" corresponds (cf. Stivers, Enfield, and Levinson 2007, 18). Adding a demonstrative pronoun to these descriptive reference forms draws focus to the form and also to the action accomplished through the use of that form (Stivers 2007). Referring to a defendant as "that criminal," therefore, highlights the lack of individual personhood conveyed by that form and the generalized characteristics that "criminal" implies.

Linguistic research and testimony such as Gobodo-Madikizela's confirms overall the centrality of language to our conceptualizations of persons and the degree of humanity we are willing to allow them. The underlying meanings of person reference, more specifically, are crucial to examine in the context of death penalty trials, as the law requires jurors to consider the individual humanity of each capital defendant (Steiker and Steiker 1995). When jurors use nonspecific, categorical reference forms in this context, they reveal a tendency to eclipse a capital defendant's individuality, despite the legal requirement to consider it.

ANALYZING DEMONSTRATIVE REFERENCE AND PROXIMITY

It is within this framework that I will analyze the use of demonstrative reference forms for referring to defendants both in trials and in jurors' postverdict interviews. While examining the many uses of demonstrative reference forms, I found that speakers most frequently referred to defendants this way when they were dehumanizing them. These acts of dehumanization were often embedded within attempts to justify, for jurors especially, sentences of death. This implies that these particular forms of reference provide sources for jurors to distance themselves from defendants in order to cast them out of their moral universe—and perhaps out of the human community[7] as a whole—in order to end their lives.

EXAMPLES OF REPAIR

Instances of repair in conversation are highly illustrative in revealing the underlying structures and meanings of language use (Schegloff 1979). Some examples of repair *into* demonstrative reference forms will thus serve here as an introduction into the conversational work they can do and their markedness[8] in contrast to other potential reference forms. In other words, instances when a speaker starts to refer to the defendant as "he," stops herself, and finishes with a demonstrative reference form are thus especially telling regarding what the demonstrative reference form in particular conveys. In the following excerpt from a juror interview, a juror

---

7. In his dissenting opinion regarding a case that upheld a death sentence that was challenged as racially biased, Justice Brennan refers to defendants sentenced to death as "[t]hose whom we would banish from society or from the human community itself" (*McClesky v. Kemp*, 481 U.S. 279, 343 (1987); Brennan, J., dissenting).

8. Markedness refers to linguistic forms that stand out as especially meaningful in relation to default or normalized alternatives. Roman Jakobson defined a marked form as "characterized by the conveyance of more precise, specific, and additional information than the unmarked term provides" (1990, 138).

responded to my question about when during the trial she started thinking about the death penalty specifically.

> 'Cause the first thing he did, he shot her in the stomach. And then we did the, that *he* was guilty, *the—this guy* doesn't have a heart. So, that's when I thought because he killed an infant in somebody's (body).

This juror commented on the crime itself ("he shot her in the stomach") and subsequently dehumanized the defendant, claiming that "this guy doesn't have a heart." After using the unmarked pronoun "he" to refer to the defendant, the juror cut off a reference form ("the—") that we might assume would have been "the defendant" or "the guy." The juror corrected herself and ultimately used the form "this guy" in her dehumanizing utterance.

This repair highlights the intensifying (e.g., Baker 1995) function of the demonstrative reference form, bringing particular focus to the defendant and to the action being accomplished through it (Stivers 2007): it dissociates the juror from the defendant, whom she depicts as nonhuman. This may be a moral distancing, in that she does not want to associate herself with such a being. It may also be a cognitive distancing, in that she cannot comprehend a person committing such an act, and thus *this guy* marks cognitive distance between herself and the referent and his associated actions. Many jurors express disbelief at the murders they are required to judge, leading jury researchers to conclude that the crime itself can often be the sole reason a juror commits a defendant to death. The juror's use of language in the previous example reveals this trend; thinking about the brutal crime led her to distance herself from the defendant as an individual person, which allowed her to consider sentencing him to death ("so that's when I thought").[9]

LEGAL MODELS OF LINGUISTIC DISTANCE

Attorneys' talk during trial serves as an authoritative model for jurors' conceptualizations of defendants. Attorneys serve as gatekeepers of law (Zacharias 2004), often acting as jurors' entryway into understanding and working through the law in their decisions. As one would expect, prosecutors aim to dehumanize defendants and often do so through their linguistic choices. The following texts present a variety of utterances from one prosecutor's closing argument, each of which includes a nonspecific reference form that distances the defendant (as referent) from his individual identity, thus dehumanizing him. In the case from which these excerpts are drawn, the defendant murdered almost an entire family, with one female child being the only survivor.

> *The person that did this* scares the hell out of her [referring to the child].

> *The person that killed like this* is extremely dangerous.

> . . . evidence to show you just who *this defendant* is

> She's [the young child] still traumatized by what *that defendant* did to her.

This prosecutor's references to the defendant utilize forms toward the right side of figure 5.1, thereby conveying the

---

9. The use of "he" in the latter part of this excerpt will be analyzed later on in the chapter.

defendant not as an identified individual, but as a generalized type, according to the crime he committed and his status as a defendant in a murder case. The first two references give the defendant status as a person, but identify him in relation to his criminal act. In the latter two examples, referring to the defendant as "defendant" defines him in terms of his categorical, legal status.

Remember that these forms appeared in the prosecutor's closing argument. They thus occurred toward the end of the trial, at which point the jurors would have already been inundated with references to the defendant and would have shared the courtroom with him for weeks if not months. The demonstrative form then, which is most often used in English to bring a new referent into focus or to remind the listener of a referent stored in their distant memory (Swierzbin 2010), would be highly marked at this point in the trial, thus highlighting these additional indexical meanings.

Rather than employing a personalized reference form, such as a name, which would denote closeness and affinity with the defendant, the prosecutor refers to him through descriptive noun phrases centered on his criminal act. The latter two instances intensify this distancing force by using the *demonstrative adjective + noun phrase* format ("that kind of person," "that individual"). In comparison to the definite article "the," "that," as a deictic form, has an added element of distance built into it. These examples thus all convey an element of distance from the defendant's "real" self (Gobodo-Madikizela 2003, 121).

In addition, in the last utterance of this series (she's [a surviving victim] still traumatized by what that defendant did to her), *that defendant* intensifies the emotional, psychic, and physical distance the victim needs to maintain from the defendant, given the traumatic experience she went through at his hands. In contrast to some accounts of deixis, according to which the demonstrative *that* indexes a referent that is no longer of interest to the speaker (e.g., Chen 1990), I argue the use of *that* intensifies focus on the referent, but in a way that heightens the affective/emotional/moral *distance* from such referent. In this example, in addition to using the heightened distancing form, *that*, the descriptor "defendant," in contrast to "guy" or "person," further severs the link between the defendant and his personal identity.

In the next example, another prosecutor used demonstrative reference in conjunction with blatantly dehumanizing language about a defendant. This example is drawn from an online news story, which was published the day a jury retired for sentencing deliberations. The prosecutor was quoted in a media interview:

> "You look for some humanity in *this defendant*. You look for some emotion, some heart, some soul in *this defendant*," said Prosecutor John Jordan. "You can watch it [the defendant's testimony] 20 times and you won't find it."[910]

Here, the prosecutor describes the defendant's utter lack of humanity, by insisting he lacks emotion, heart, and soul, punctuating this by referring to him as "this defendant." Even when the jury heard his own voice during his testimony, the prosecutor claims, his humanity did not come through.

Demonstrative reference thus serves as a potent rhetorical device for prosecutors, especially, to create emotional and

10. ABC Eyewitness News online, "Jury decides cop killer's punishment," May 21, 2008. http://abclocal.go.com/story?section=news/local&id=6154374.

moral distance between defendants and jurors. The following examples are drawn from a prosecutor's penalty closing argument. The prosecutor did not refer to the defendant at all in the first portion of his address, referring to the crime instead and its details, eliding any named offender. In contrast, he continually used proper names to refer to the *victims*, specifying their personal individuality and thus bringing them, as individuals, into the jurors' focus. For example, he described a picture of the crime scene:

> It shows you part of what this crime was about, the why this crime was committed. Think back on the pictures of that closet and how there was blood spatter all the way from the hallway . . . remember the way the drawers looked in *Fred Simmons'* room.

The victim is the only named individual in this depiction, as the defendant's identity in the criminal actions is omitted. Throughout the rest of his argument, the prosecutor referred to the defendant in the following ways (this is not a complete list of his references to the defendant, but illustrates the general trend):

> It's opened because *the defendant* is looking for things to take.
>
> What *Derrick Jackson* has done is not their fault.
>
> It's not called the what is best for *Derrick Jackson* phase.
>
> . . . was all about *the defendant* getting a fair trial
>
> *The person that did this* scares the hell out of her.
>
> *That kind of person* would be capable of doing all of this again.
>
> *The person that killed like this* is extremely dangerous.
>
> *The person that did this* is not polite.
>
> There is nothing shy about *that kind of individual*.

The person that committed these crimes, there is nothing reserved about *that individual* at all.

There sits in the room with you right now *the most dangerous deadly person* you will ever know.

As seen in this partial list of the prosecutor's reference choices, his argument began with reference to the defendant either as such or with his proper name, both relatively specified on a scale of determinacy, as the definite article "the" is a relatively specific reference form in contrast to less specified markers such as indefinite articles and pronouns (DuBois 1980). The prosecutor then transformed his references to the defendant, increasingly using less definite identifiers, often in the form of demonstrative noun phrases or descriptive noun phrases, such as *that kind of person, that kind of individual, the person that did this,* and *the person that committed these crimes.* These forms serve to forsake the defendant as an individual and instead foreground his criminal actions. Even in the final reference, when the prosecutor individually pointed out the defendant in the courtroom, he concomitantly referred to the defendant not by his name, but as a "person," indexing not his individuality, but his dangerousness: "the most dangerous deadly person you will ever know."

During arguments such as these, jurors are guided to think of the defendant not as a person, but as a token of a rare type—the exceptionally violent. The consistent use of these forms thus encourages the perspective that the defendant's personhood is hopelessly tied up with his criminality and status as a capital defendant. This leaves little room for potential change and rehabilitation, thus decreasing the likelihood that jurors will be swayed to a life sentence by any potentially mitigating evidence.

JURORS, DEMONSTRATIVE REFERENCE, AND GIVING DEATH

Whether through conscious evocation of attorneys' language or not, jurors reproduced these demonstrative reference forms when speaking of defendants during their posttrial interviews. They, too, used these forms when dehumanizing defendants, and in turn, in justifying their decisions for death. This often occurred when jurors discussed the future danger of defendants, and, in some cases, expressed fear that they would get out of prison at some point. For instance, in the following example, a juror justified his decision for death, specifically explaining his rationale for voting yes to the future danger question:

> I would hate to be the guy that turned *this guy* loose because we thought, well, maybe in forty years he'll be, *he'll be a good boy.*

Here the demonstrative reference form was used in a hypothetical depiction of the defendant if he is let out of prison. The juror feared that letting "this guy loose," as if the defendant were an animal in a cage, would allow him to hurt more people in the future. This demonstrative reference form is contrasted to the juror's ironic reference to a "good boy," in which the personal pronoun "he" was used. The point, of course, is that the defendant will never be a good boy, and thus deserves to have his life eliminated. This example also provides an interesting case in which the juror refers to himself as "the guy," depersonalizing his own involvement in this process (see chapter 6).

The concern that capital defendants would someday get out of prison loomed large for many jurors, especially in assessing their answer to whether the defendant would be a future danger to society. Additionally, many jurors inaccurately assumed that life without parole still might leave room for the defendant to be paroled in the future, thus convincing them that execution was the only way to ensure the defendant would not be released from prison.

DEHUMANIZATION AND DEATH SENTENCES

Classifying someone as nonhuman is often cited as a technique that allows a person to kill another human being (e.g., Grossman 2009). Jurors often talked of defendants as nonhuman, lacking essential human characteristics, such as a heart or emotions. Not surprisingly, these explicit acts of dehumanization often entailed use of demonstrative reference forms. Recall the juror quoted previously who started to consider the death penalty when she found the defendant guilty. A person who could commit such a crime, in her mind, is not a person at all.

> 'Cause the first thing he did, he shot her in the stomach. And then we did the, that he was guilty, the—*this guy doesn't have a heart.*

In this context, the demonstrative construction "this guy," as opposed to other potential referential forms, such as "he," distances the juror from the defendant and positions him as distinct from other, normal persons. "This guy" occupies the subject role in the literal dehumanization of the defendant—"doesn't have a heart." Using an unmarked reference form in this context, such as the personal pronoun "he," would be consistent with a picture of the referent as unremarkable, fitting into normal social categories. But this defendant, having shot a pregnant woman in the stomach, arguably should not be included in those categories.

The following excerpt, drawn from another juror's interview, illustrates even more explicitly the discursive construction of defendants as beings outside of normal categories of persons.

> A normal person wouldn't have done what he did, and you see *this guy* that is kind of nonemotional either direction, and you see him as kind of as *not as a normal person.* Not that he's crazy, but that it's just like, he could, he was totally separated from—from what you'd think normal emotions would be.

The distance created through the demonstrative reference form "this guy" parallels this juror's conceptualization of metaphoric distance between the defendant and other "normal" persons: "he was totally separated from . . . normal emotions." As seen in chapter 4, jurors like this one often react to defendants' apparent lack of emotion as evidence of their lack of humanity. This logic again identifies the defendant not as an individual, but as a member of a type—one that is exempt from the category of "normal" persons.

As argued above, dehumanization acts as one step toward a juror or any potential killer transforming a person into an entity whose life is dispensable. Demonstrative reference forms contribute to linguistic acts of dehumanization, allowing jurors to justify ending a defendant's life. The following juror's proclamation exhibited this logic:

> You think, well, *that person,* you know, they just need to be, you know, eliminated.

This juror used the more distancing form "that" when talking about the ultimate denial of empathy with another—claiming that "that person" needs to be eliminated. On a continuum of deictic proximity, *that* distances the referent further than *this* from the deictic *origo*, often defined as the speaker's inner or affective world (Caffi and Janney 1994, 364), thus implying emotional detachment from the referent (Lakoff 1974). This juror thus exhibited the primary concern of this book, how language can help make death decisions possible.

DEMONSTRATIVE REFERENCE AND JURORS' ATTRIBUTION OF CRIMINAL RESPONSIBILITY

In his account of an "empathic divide" between jurors and defendants in death penalty trials, Haney (2004) posits that the less similar jurors and defendants are to one another, the less likely it is a juror will experience empathy toward a defendant. He further argues that as the similarity between jurors and defendants decreases, jurors are more likely to attribute *internal* causes to defendants' behavior rather than *external* ones. He relies on attribution theory in this analysis, which asserts that causal attributions about others' behavior can be explained in two ways: by "internal dispositions and willful choices of the actor, or . . . external circumstances and conditions over which the actor has less control" (Haney 2004, 1580). Internal causes are behaviors thought to be products of the defendant's free will, such as choosing to get drunk, while external causes include forces not under the defendant's control, such as his race or his family background. Interestingly and often unfortunately for many capital defenders, mental illnesses are often considered by jurors as intermediary between internal and external causes, making them tricky to argue as convincingly mitigating factors against harsh sentencing.

Haney contends that when jurors explain defendants' crimes in terms of internal causes, they are more likely to hold them personally responsible and punish them more harshly (Haney 2004, 1581). Using this position as a starting point, this section examines demonstrative reference forms, analyzing the grammatical role a given referent serves in an utterance. In other words, when jurors use demonstrative forms to refer to defendants, is the form the agent or the object of the action described? Is the defendant as "that guy" positioned grammatically as in control of his criminal actions, or is he acting at the will of some external force? How do these reference forms therefore correspond with jurors' theories of defendants' criminal culpability?

Among instances of demonstrative reference to defendants in jurors' interviews, the majority of those used when talking about the defendant's *crime* take the agent role in an utterance. In contrast, those used when talking about the defendant's *punishment*, specifically jurors' involvement in it, maintain the patient role. In the cases of talk about the defendant's criminal behavior, the defendant was overwhelmingly portrayed as being individually responsible for his actions, which falls under Haney's (2004) category of internal causation. Consider the following examples, in which jurors discussed defendants' criminal behavior:

JUROR 1: *That man's* been committing crimes since he was thirteen years old.

JUROR 2: *This defendant* went on and on [bludgeoning the victims].

JUROR 3: When *this defendant* left that apartment...

JUROR 4: *This guy* made an escape and hurt somebody.

JUROR 5: *This guy's* just killed six people.

JUROR 6: *This person* knowingly and intentionally ran into that guard.

In these utterances, the defendant is referenced through demonstrative forms (*that man, this defendant, this guy, this person*) and conveyed as the agent of predicates that portray a number of dangerous behaviors. The grammatical agency in these utterances conveys each defendant as responsible for committing the acts described. Jurors' portrayals of culpability thus tend to correspond with Haney's analysis: as jurors established distance between themselves and defendants, indexing lack of empathy with them through the demonstrative reference form, they positioned them grammatically as individually responsible for their actions. In all of these cases, the jurors sentenced the defendants to death, thus punishing them more harshly as Haney would predict.

Seemingly counter to this argument, there are some cases when the unmarked, personal pronoun "he" was used when jurors spoke of defendants' criminal behavior. Instances such as this, I argue, serve to individualize defendants precisely when their responsibility for their crimes is at stake. Thus while jurors may wish to distance themselves from defendants when talking about their almost unspeakable crimes, as in "This guy's just killed six people," they may also highlight the defendant's individual responsibility for the crime, thus producing the alternative form, "He just killed six people."

In his exploration of the interpersonal space created through deixis and the conditional tense, Haverkate describes "defocalization," a distancing technique whereby a speaker, through indeterminate reference to himself, distances himself from his role in the actions or state of affairs described in an utterance (1992, 516). For instance, the nonspecific pronoun "one" can suppress the identity of participants in an action, thus eliding the speaker's individual responsibility for such action.

As I have shown elsewhere, prosecutors often used demonstrative forms when referencing defendants, which create moral distance between themselves, jurors, and defendants. However, there are cases in which prosecutors used the unmarked and more specified reference form "he" or the even more specified proper name when referring to defendants. This often occurred when attorneys described the defendants' intentional criminal behavior. The personal pronoun or proper name, I argue in line with Haverkate, is used in these contexts to maintain the defendant's individual responsibility for the events being described. Using the demonstrative reference—a less individualized form—in these cases would potentially mitigate such a role. In the following example, a prosecutor describes a defendant's confession to criminal action:

> The theft of the Camaro. When *Mr. Michael Johnson* admitted to going back to the Stotler residence and stealing the Camaro.

In this example, drawn from a prosecutor's punishment phase closing statement, the prosecutor used a reference form that is highly remarkable in this context because of its overt violation of the preference for minimization (Schegloff 1979). This form, which comes subsequent to numerous references to the defendant throughout the attorney's argument, is highly individualized (toward the left endpoint of figure 5.1), intensified by the use of the first name within a form usually reserved for last name only (Mr. Johnson).

So why use such a personalized, specified form, when the prosecutor wishes to create interpersonal distance between himself, the jury, and the defendant? This hyperspecified form is used in conjunction with an explicit mention of the defendant's intentional criminal behavior—behavior he admitted to committing. Using an unspecified form in this case would mitigate the defendant's involvement in the action, which would contradict the force and meaning of the utterance—the defendant's direct responsibility for stealing the car and admitting that he did so.

A similar example occurred in a prosecutor's punishment closing argument from a different case. Throughout his argument, the prosecutor capitalized on the negative stance demonstrative reference forms can index, frequently referring to the defendant as "this defendant." He switched to the defendant's proper name in the following utterance, however:

What *David Johnson* has done is not [his family's] responsibility.

Again, in speaking of the defendant's culpability for the crime, the highly specified proper name is used for reference to him. Specifically, he is named as an individual in order to distinguish him as personally responsible for the crime, as opposed to his family sharing in the blame.

The following provides an additional example of the impact using the defendant's name can have on highlighting his criminal culpability. This excerpt is also drawn from the above prosecutor's punishment phase closing argument:

> You get to know the real *David Johnson*. And here you get to take into consideration his victims, the impact on the victims' family and society.

In attempting to convince the jury of his "real" nature, which revolves around criminal behavior, the prosecutor personally identifies the defendant with his full name (cf. Gobodo-Madikizela 2003). This is a highly unusual practice for prosecutors in general. They tend to use less humanizing reference forms, such as the demonstrative forms described in this chapter, while defense attorneys make an effort to always refer to the defendant by name. Prosecutors will, however, refer to victims using their proper names to humanize them to juries. In the example above, in contrast, the *victims* remain unspecified, and in fact are only specified in the sense of being "his" (belonging to the defendant), thus intensifying the defendant's involvement in the acts of killing them.

Returning to the juror above who denied her defendant a heart, we can see the same shift in reference form when she alludes to the defendant's crime:

> the—*this guy* doesn't have a heart. So, that's when I thought because *he* killed an infant in somebody's (body).

Though her overall point here is that because of the unthinkable crime the defendant committed, he lacks a central component of what it means to be a human, she used a more personalized reference form—*he*—potentially to highlight the defendant's responsibility for that unthinkable act.

In summary, while I found an occasional correlation between jurors' distancing stances toward defendants and their attributions of internal causation for their criminal behavior, jurors also used reference forms to highlight the individual personhood of defendants when discussing their personal responsibility for their crimes. This corresponds with findings from other death penalty scholars, which suggest that capital jurors often disregard mitigating evidence as irrelevant to their sentencing decisions, using instead the defendant's crime as their primary rationalization for giving death.

THIS GUY'S LIFE IS AT STAKE

Though the instances are relatively rare in both my trial and interview data, jurors and attorneys occasionally used the demonstrative form "this guy" when establishing a positive stance toward defendants. As shown in figure 5.1, *this* lies on the intimacy side of the continuum in comparison to its deictic opposite, *that*. Both, however, convey relative distance in contrast to other forms, such as proper names. In the following cases, the use of the demonstrative as a marked reference term serves to highlight the speaker's affective involvement with the defendant, which, in these cases, is positive rather than negative (Ostman 1995, 257). The distal form *that*, however, was *never* used in a context in which positive affect was being evoked. So, returning yet again to the question—*Why that now?*—what does the proximal deictic form *this* do in jurors' references to defendants in contexts of positive, rather than the more common negative, emotional stances?

In comparing the discursive contexts of these instances, I found that jurors and attorneys utilized "this guy" when referencing the defendant's life being at stake. Thus in those moments when jurors did reflect on the fact that an individual's life is literally in the balance, they used the demonstrative *this* potentially to bring the defendant closer, as it were, conveying an empathetic stance with him. At the same time, the juror may use the demonstrative *this*, rather than choosing a more intimate form toward the left of figure 5.1, in order to maintain distance between himself and the potential act of actually taking another person's life. The following excerpts from juror interviews exhibit this phenomenon:

JUROR 1: And *this guy*, I mean if we're going to err we're gonna err on the side of life.

JUROR 2: It obviously makes you think about life and death, and you know *this guy* is twenty-eight, or however old he was . . . *this guy* who's got to make his life right with God.

In this context, the deictic *this* can be seen as possibly distancing the juror from the defendant in order to better cope, even in his interview reflections, with the unbearably heavy burden of ending another's life. However, when viewed against its contrastive form, *that, this*, as the proximal deictic form, is generally used when a speaker identifies somehow with the referent (Cornish 2001). Thus we can also view these examples as times when a juror, in talking about a defendant's life, identifies with him, bringing him close, as it were, to himself, thus invoking empathy with him.

This function is further intensified through the form "this kid" and similar variations, which were used more commonly in the context of positive alignment with defendants than "this guy" or "this man." By incorporating the diminutive version of the descriptor "guy," "this kid" further marks each juror's empathy with defendants.

JUROR 1: *This kid* came from a rough family.

JUROR 2: What could we have done earlier on in *this kid's* life, you know, what do you do to make sure the other kids don't do that?

JUROR 3: You know, here he is. *This kid's* on, you know, on trial for his life.

JUROR 4: Well, the prosecutors started from *this young man's* very youthful life, in which, you know, he was adopted. They suggested that the mother might've been on drugs when she was pregnant. Who knows how or what affected him.

Juror 1 expressed sympathy with the defendant, considering the evidence about his family life as potentially mitigating. The reference form "this kid" in this context indexes a stance of empathy toward the defendant, which may index his feeling that this rough family may be a reason to spare the defendant's life. For Jurors 2 and 3, the defendant's life was again the topic of discussion; the jurors expressed uneasiness about harsh sentencing, the first questioning what could have stopped the defendant's criminal behavior in the first place, the second reflecting on the defendant's life being at stake. In both of these examples, *this kid* again intensifies each juror's affective stance toward the defendants, ultimately expressing sympathy for them. Last, Juror 4 again describes mitigating evidence, using a similar diminutive form, "this young man," in discussing the potential ramifications of the defendant's mother's drug use during pregnancy on his life. We again get a sense from the diminutive reference form that the juror took seriously this evidence as potential mitigation against a death sentence.

Again, we must ask why the demonstrative forms, rather than a more individualized form such as a first name, were used in these contexts of positive affect. One possible explanation is that the defendants were still being identified as tokens of a particular type. Though the jurors were expressing positive stances toward the defendants, encouraging empathy with them, the demonstrative form could possibly have been used because jurors still saw them as one of many individuals who come from bad families or whose lives are on trial. This is often the logic I was given when I asked jurors why a particular piece of mitigating evidence was not deemed *sufficiently* mitigating in order to give the defendant a life sentence. Jurors provided responses along the lines of, "Well, I know this defendant had a bad family life and was addicted to drugs, but so are a lot of people. And not all of them go out and kill somebody, so why should he be let off the hook?" All the jurors quoted in the previous excerpts in fact sentenced their defendants to death, making this explanation especially plausible.

REFERENCE FORMS AS INDICATORS OF LIFE OR DEATH DECISIONS

As explained in chapter 2, none of the jurors I interviewed were pro-life for their defendants, even though one of the juries as a whole voted for life. My own data therefore cannot provide a reliable correlation between jurors' use of reference forms and a particular sentencing verdict. When reading through other accounts of capital jurors' decisions, however, I did find a correlation. Interviews with capital jurors excerpted in Fleury-Steiner's *Jurors' Stories of Death* (2004), for instance, reveal that jurors who voted for life indeed tended to refer to defendants with reference forms located toward the left side of figure 5.1, such as first names. These jurors also tended to display more empathy with defendants. The excerpts below, drawn from Fleury-Steiner's juror interviews as published, illustrate this pattern (I have selected a small number to show here, though many more could be cited that fall within this pattern). In introducing these excerpts, Fleury-Steiner describes them as examples of expressions of empathy and mercy towards defendants:

JUROR 1: *David* hadn't been given the chance that [another defendant] had been given. . . . See, *David's* father taught him to steal. . . . I think that was probably partly what allowed me to say, "Yes, I think he should be given life in prison." (76)

JUROR 2: I know *Mark* knew better, and he knew what he was doing was wrong. But he doesn't deserve the death penalty. (77)

JUROR 3: We have a very loving family, so it's really different than *Mark's* upbringing. I mean, *Mark* was out all hours of the night. (77)

In the following example, in contrast to many of the jurors I spoke with quoted above, this juror—who also voted for life—linguistically downplays the defendant's responsibility for his crime, while developing an empathic stance toward him based on his troubled childhood:

I can't imagine anyone on that jury who was not affected by *the crime, Morris Green's* childhood, and by the incredible work that went on in the jury room. (80)

The juror here nominalizes "the crime," eliminating reference to any human agent involved. He then personalizes the defendant through his given name, thus depicting empathy with him when speaking of the horrendous childhood he lived through.

Fleury-Steiner's jurors who voted for death, on the other hand, overwhelmingly used distancing forms when referencing defendants, especially the demonstrative forms described in this chapter. In the following example, a juror dehumanizes the defendant as many of my jurors did, citing his lack of emotional displays during trial (see chapter 4). In line with jurors quoted above, moreover, this juror uses the demonstrative reference form when describing his fear that the defendant will "get out," again likening him to a caged animal.[11]

> He didn't bat an eye, not a tear, no emotion at all. That pretty much put him in the electric chair. . . . I was very concerned that *this guy* could get out of prison. I mean, with his episodes of violence . . . (94–95)

In the course of their interviews, jurors are justifying their decisions—often described as the most difficult of their lives—to their interviewer and to themselves. If justifying life sentences, jurors frequently describe feeling empathy for defendants, often referencing specific mitigating evidence to explain why. In these instances, reference forms aid jurors in the empathic stance they wish to convey. When justifying death sentences, on the other hand, jurors often deny that

---

11. Though there is not room to reproduce them here, many examples of these particular references to defendants can be found in Sundby's *A Life and Death Decision* (2005) as well.

defendants are human at all. Reference forms again aid jurors in this process. Language, therefore, plays a significant role in jurors working through these justifications; linguistic choices serve to navigate their empathizing with or dehumanizing defendants.

REFERENCE AND DEFENDANTS' HUMANITY

This chapter has demonstrated the subtle but crucial actions that reference forms can help speakers accomplish in the context of death penalty trials. Reference forms, in that they always convey something about a speaker's stance toward the person being referred to, reveal much about how jurors and attorneys linguistically—and actually—determine defendants' lives.

I present a final example to convey this crucial relationship between language and the relative degrees of humanity afforded to capital defendants. It is drawn from an interview with a juror who is unique, not in the sense that he voted for death, but because after the trial he became an activist of sorts, speaking in a variety of venues about the need for life without parole, an option his jury wished would have been available to them but was not at the time of his the trial. He also visited the defendant, Bobby Jackson, in prison after the trial's conclusion and has remained in contact with him, which is extremely rare. He thus had much greater personal familiarity with the defendant than most other jurors did. This excerpt, in which the juror reflected on the reality of making a life-and-death decision, illustrates an interplay of relations of physical proximity with deictically marked discursive relationships, and the consequences both have for this jurors' experience of empathy.

> When you're confronted with it, it's not like anything I could have ever imagined, because you read newspaper accounts or you watch on TV and *you think*, well, *that person, you know, they just need to be, you know, eliminated*. And let me tell you, from the graphic pictures we saw, this would fall [laughing] in that category. But, you know, then you realize there's *a real human being*. Did *he* stumble, fall, and even if *he* did, just the mere fact of loading a shotgun and putting *somebody* in that position—I mean, is that, that's pretty serious! . . . It was very interesting to meet *Bobby*, and *he's* a very gentle soul, and *we*, as *Bobby* says, *we're* two sides of the same coin. *We* were educated probably within a mile and a half of each other. And, you know, *we* knew the same streets and things like that. When you start talking about it, it's like frightening [laughing] *how close we all are*. And *this is as far as you think two people would be*. But then you start to see the similarities. That's truly interesting.

In this example, the juror's deictic terms mirror his ruminations about physical proximity between people and the inevitable sense of similarity that derives from it. That sense of similarity allows him to empathize with this particular defendant (spurring, we might assume, his attempts to make contact with the defendant after the sentence). His linguistic choices mark shifts between displaying social closeness and empathy with the individual defendant and distance and lack of empathy with the class of people who commit similar crimes. At first, the juror invoked a normalized view that anyone who commits murder should be "eliminated" and that such an act is not commensurate with "imaginable" categories of actions. In this typological classification, the referent is "that person," "that" distancing the hypothetical criminal from the juror. In making such a potentially inflammatory statement, that someone be eliminated, this juror also distanced himself from the telling, by using the indefinite and generalized subject "you" rather than "I" ("you think . . ."). This linguistic distancing, accomplished through a decrease in specification of the subject, allows the juror to evade responsibility for the statement and, by extension, for the potential act of elimination.

There followed a phenomenological shift, whereby the juror moved from referencing a type of criminal to identifying the defendant as a "real human being," not merely an unnamed member of the group just alluded to. Immediately following this description, the juror switched from the demonstrative phrase "that guy" to using the pronoun "he": "did he stumble, fall, and even if he did." This switch to "he" shifted the juror's alignment to his new referent—the defendant as a person—and evokes empathy with him. The juror then alluded to the crime, as the defendant loaded his shotgun and pointed it at "somebody." While the defendant is individualized, the victim is anonymized here, referred to as "somebody." The linguistic and experiential closeness resides between the juror and the defendant (and, by extension, me as the listener), while the victim remains distanced through the indefinite pronoun.

The juror further positioned the defendant as an actual person when referencing their face-to-face meeting. He referred to him most intimately, with his first name: Bobby. With this name, he invoked Bobby specifically, bringing him into the room, as it were, by reporting his words ("as Bobby says"). He then employed the inclusive pronoun "we" to describe their similar upbringings. Their geographic proximity as children allowed the juror to recognize their commonalities and shared knowledge and facilitated empathic understanding with Bobby's situation. Despite the differences in the moral boundaries of this juror's and defendant's typical actions, prompting the juror to state that "this is as far as you think two people would be," he found closeness to the defendant based in their growing up within a mile and a half of each other. He concluded with a generalization about humanity based in proximity, that it's "frightening . . . how close we all are."

Returning to the problem posed at the beginning of the chapter, we can see that particular linguistic choices, through their management of speakers' proximity to defendants, can stymie empathy with defendants and justify jurors' decisions for death. Specifically, varieties in person reference, such as demonstrative noun phrases, when used in various discourse contexts, can operate as both distancing and inclusive tactics among jurors, attorneys, and defendants.

Deictic expressions, as mediators of proximity among people, discursive content, and context, are thus indispensable for understanding empathic relationships and the link between language and psychological processes more generally. There is a demonstrable parallelism between the "intersubjectively shared external world of social processes and the subjective internal world of individual affective process" (Caffi and Janney 1994, 365). In this sense, both persons and their language are subjective: the subjectivity of an utterance is, as Lyons proposes, the speaker's "expression of himself in the act of the utterance" (1982, 240; cf. Ochs 2012), which is encoded through the speaker's specific linguistic choices, such as those displayed above. It is in this sense that language is inseparable from our understanding of the subjective experiences of persons and especially how these are related to and constituted through our perceptual access to others. It follows logically that legal decision-making—itself made of language—is inseparable from these subjective experiences as well. Moreover, language scholars such as Hanks (1990) and philosophers such as Husserl (1969) remind us that both deixis and empathy are oriented to the speaking and feeling ego; the other is always emplaced and understood through the self (and vice versa). Thus jurors hold an extreme degree of power, in that the defendant's character and fate, while partially located in his own embodied action, is sifted through the jurors' own subjectivities and experiences.

The analyses in this chapter provide a linguistic model of the degree to which attorneys and, most importantly, jurors judge defendants according to their "real" selves. Language, itself a system of categorization, provides ample resources to identify people according to types—to elide their individual characteristics in favor of attributes that connect them to some particular group of persons. Language can also enable empathy, however; it can individualize persons, as Gobodo-Madikizela and the jurors who voted for life reveal. Texas death penalty law requires that jurors move beyond seeing defendants as tokens of a type, however. The taking of an individual life requires that jurors examine this life, including all its moral and experiential vicissitudes. Language can both facilitate and disrupt this process.

6

Agents of the State: Capital Jurors' Accountability for Death Sentences

TO WHAT EXTENT DO CAPITAL jurors recognize and admit that they are directly involved in a process in which a person may die? This chapter explores how jurors conceptualize their roles in death penalty administration, asking whether and how capital trials transform laypeople into state killers. Language is a critical facilitator of this transformation. This chapter argues that Texas's special issue framework, as expressed in jurors' instructions and attorneys' talk during voir dire, allows and in fact guides jurors to avoid their responsibility for defendants' death sentences, and, ultimately, for their deaths.[1] The chapter analyzes grammatical constructions of agency in particular as contributing to jurors' mitigations of responsibility for their death penalty decisions. I conclude that jurors' willingness or unwillingness to sentence another human being to death is facilitated in large part by their socialization into authoritative, institutional models of capital sentencing.

1. Weiner et al. 2004; Garvey 2000; Joseph L. Hoffman 1995.

As reviewed previously, Texas's unique post-*Furman* sentencing schema was established to urge jurors to consider defendants' individual lives more thoroughly when making their sentencing decisions.[2] In practice, however, the schema achieves a different result; it facilitates jurors' *minimal* consideration of defendants' lives and deaths. The precise language of the special issue questions, reproduced below, contributes significantly to jurors' understandings of their roles in defendants' deaths.

1. Do you find from the evidence beyond a reasonable doubt that there is a probability that the defendant would commit criminal acts of violence that would constitute a continuing threat to society?

2. Do you find from the evidence, taking into consideration all of the evidence, including the circumstances of the offense, the defendant's character and background, and the personal moral culpability of the defendant, that there is a sufficient mitigating circumstance or circumstances to warrant that a sentence of life imprisonment rather than a death sentence be imposed?

I reiterate that in this sentencing schema, jurors never pronounce specifically whether they sentence a defendant to life in prison or death. They merely answer these two questions, which instruct a judge as to how the defendant should be sentenced. This procedure guides jurors to deny responsibility for sending defendants to their deaths (cf. Vartkessian, Sorensen, and Kelly 2014).

2. *Woodson v. North Carolina*, 428 U.S. at 303, Gregg v. Georgia 428 US 153 (1976), *Proffit v. Florida* 428 US 242 (1976), *Jurek v. Texas* 428 US 262 (1976).

RESPONSIBILITY AND THE DEATH PENALTY

A tremendous amount of time and a wide array of actors contribute to accomplishing an execution in the United States.[3] Throughout the process of taking a person's life (which for many defendants takes several years, beginning the day they are sentenced and spanning the years during which appeals are submitted, finally ending in their actual execution), jurors, judges, and prison staff consider themselves variously accountable for the event as a whole. Many limit their involvement to specific contributory acts, such as strapping the prisoner's right arm to the gurney, or reading a sentencing verdict aloud to a courtroom's occupants. Processing one's position on the "path of death" (Osofsky, Bandura, and Zimbardo 2005, 385), at whatever stage, arguably requires "mechanisms of moral disengagement" (Osofsky, Bandura, and Zimbardo 2005, 372; cf. Haney 1997; Lynch and Haney 2011a; 2011b; Milgram 1974), which include, for instance, dehumanizing the victim (Haney 1997) and distributing responsibility for the act among multiple people, both of which are theorized as necessary steps to killing in many contexts (Grossman 2004; 2009; Haritos-Fatouros 2002; Huggins, Haritos-Fatouros, and Zimbardo 2002; Waller 2002). In the case of US capital punishment, responsibility for carrying out a lethal injection, for instance, is often distributed among members of a team of prison staff, ensuring that an executioner is not required to

3. Texans, including jurors and attorneys, often boast that Texas operates the most efficient capital punishment system in the U.S. I heard many times during my fieldwork that Texas is "not like California," which is reportedly notorious for drawing out the execution process.

bear individual responsibility for killing a capital offender (Eisenberg, Garvey, and Wells 1996, 339).

In addition, the "spectacle" of the death penalty has, in the last two centuries, been transported from the public execution to the courtroom, thus bureaucratizing the violence inherent to the process (Sarat 1995, 1107). This movement has included transforming the death penalty into a predominantly discursive process (Sarat 1995; Garvey 2000; Osofsky, Bandura, and Zimbardo 2005, 387)—as opposed to an overtly violent one—which has arguably "desensitized" those involved to the act of killing it entails (Osofsky, Bandura, and Zimbardo 2005, 88). For many actors on this path to death, this decreases a sense of their individual accountability for executions, which is often described as "simply [carrying] out the order of the state" or the "law" (Osofsky, Bandura, and Zimbardo 2005).

Capital jurors' responsibility for an inmate's death is especially ambiguous, as they are greatly removed physically, temporally, and procedurally from the actual execution. The law has taken steps to remedy this ambiguity. Since the reimplementation of the death penalty in 1976, the Supreme Court has emphasized the need for capital jurors to recognize and act with "due regard for the consequences of their decision" *(McGautha v. California, 302 U.S. 183 (1971))*. The Eighth Amendment's "need for reliability in the determination that death is the appropriate punishment in a specific case" (*Woodson v. North Carolina, 428 U.S. 280 (Woodson v. North Carolina, 428 U.S. 280 (1976) (plurality opinion))* has been similarly interpreted to insist that jurors remain aware of the "awesome responsibility" (*McGautha*) of deciding on a defendant's life or death. In a 1985 decision, the Supreme Court strengthened this position, finding it unconstitutional for a jury to believe that the "responsibility for determining the appropriateness of the defendant's death rests elsewhere" (*Caldwell v. Mississippi, 472 U.S. 320 (Caldwell v. Mississippi, 472 U.S. 320 (1985))*.

Texas's response to these conditions—the special issue questions—has produced results that may contradict the spirit, if not the letter, of the Supreme Court's decisions. Rather than ensuring that jurors carefully consider their role in sentencing capital defendants, the special issue questions have obscured jurors' individual accountability for death sentences and their material consequences (cf. Haney 1984; Sarat 1995; Vartkessian, Sorensen, and Kelly 2014). Systematized sentencing guidelines such as Texas's special issue questions afford a death sentence "the illusion of a legal rule, so that no actor at any point in the penalty procedure need feel he has chosen to kill any individual" (Weisberg 1983, 393). From jury selection to the rendering of a verdict, jurors are socialized to a worldview in which killing is "reduced to a rule-governed event, barely resembling an act of killing at all" (Sarat 1995). The extent to which the violence of the execution itself is shrouded during capital trials contributes to many jurors' tendencies to treat it as something other than an act of killing. For those jurors who enter voir dire not thinking they could ever sentence another person to death, the procedure under which they do so in Texas makes such an act appear much more feasible.

Language, as the primary vehicle of law's power and action (Mertz 1994), is central to jurors' mitigation of responsibility for their sentencing decisions. The forthcoming sections analyze the precise linguistic mechanisms by which the translation of legal rules into a juror's denial of responsibility for her sentencing decision is accomplished. Deciding to take another life is filtered through legal language that stifles the inevitability, reality, and violence of the execution (Sarat 1995), thus performing a portion of the moral distancing required for many jurors to take the life of another human being (Haney 1997). At moments akin to clouds parting, however, jurors from my study, at various points throughout the course of a trial and after, experienced unavoidable glimpses into the violence and reality of their decisions. For some, these glimpses came in time to excuse themselves from the process entirely. For others, these arrived as retrospective feelings of guilt, often leading to troubling bouts of remorse for their involvement in sentencing a defendant to death.

LANGUAGE AND AGENCY

Language is a primary "technolog[y] through which power and social structure can be sustained and renegotiated" (Duranti 1994, 139; cf. Foucault 1977). Legal language is an especially potent technology of power, as the state's authority over knowledge and, in the case of the death penalty, over life, is made possible in large part through law's language (Mertz 1994, 446; cf. Lazarus-Black and Hirsch 1994). Importantly, this authority is unstable because it is carried out through the actions of a variety of persons with differential relationships to the law.

In discussing jurors' agency in acts of killing, it is important to be clear about what exactly I mean by agency. In linguistics, the term *agency* has a unique definition that developed independently of the sociological concept (Duranti 2001). A grammatical "agent" is an entity that carries out the action of a transitive verb (a verb that can take an object) (e.g., Dixon 1994), which action has some effect on the agent or another entity (Duranti 2001; Lyons 1977; Jackendoff 1990). In English, agents typically occupy the subject position of a sentence

(Jackendoff 1972, 32, 42), though this is not always the case (Duranti 2001), as illustrated in the following examples. In both sentences, "the judge" is the agent; however, the judge is the subject only in sentence (a).

(a) The judge sentenced the defendant.
(b) The defendant was sentenced by the judge.

Each of the world's languages has some way to encode agency grammatically, as well as structural means for its mitigation (Duranti 2001, 460). Different ways of encoding agency, as evidenced in the sentences above, can either highlight or reduce an entity's engagement in or responsibility for an action. For instance, sentence (b) downgrades the judge's responsibility for the action of sentencing by using the passive voice to place the judge at the end of the sentence, thus taking focus off them as the doer of the action. The passive voice can thus serve to diminish an entity's agency in the action described by the sentence (Ehrlich 2001, 39–40; Henle, Miller, and Beazley 1995; LaFrance and Hahn 1994). The passive voice in English also allows an agent to be deleted from a sentence altogether, as in the following: "In the U.S., a woman is raped every 6 minutes" (Ehrlich 2001, 39, adopted from Henley, Miller, and Beazley 1995). Here the person responsible for the act of rape is erased entirely, leaving the impression that no specific agent carried out the action.

While there is no simple one-to-one correlation between grammatical agency and its social counterpart, this chapter integrates these two perspectives, as many linguistic anthropologists have done (cf. Duranti 2004; 1994; Ahearn 2001; 1999; Ehrlich 2001; Rymes 1995). The examples below demonstrate how actors in capital trials, specifically jurors, both interpret and use language as a means to shape their agency in the world. When examining attributions of agency by jurors and other legal actors, one must keep in mind that they are operating within the power-laden context of a capital trial. As a result, individual agency is inescapably entangled with formidable ideologies about civic duty, state control, and moral notions of crime and justice and therefore is never solely "individual" (cf. Eisenberg, Garvey, and Wells 1996). As will be illustrated in the analyses below, grammatical agents in the context of capital trials often take institutional form in "the law" or "the state," thus inscribing in talk the power of the legal institution to affect human choices and actions. The linguistic options available in English provide a whole spectrum of means for expressing varied degrees of agency, often allowing jurors to couch their individual accountability within institutional actions.

To probe how jurors progressively conceive of their agency for death sentences throughout a trial and beyond, the following sections work chronologically through jurors' trial experiences. I begin with a discussion of the Texas sentencing scheme in general, analyzing its impact on jurors' mitigated accountability for sentencing defendants. This includes a critical examination of the written instructions that jurors receive and their ambiguous directives regarding jurors' responsibility for the outcome of their verdicts. Next, I discuss the capital voir dire as a socializing process, through which jurors are socialized into particular ways of understanding their roles in death sentences. Lastly, jurors' postverdict reflections about their experiences reveal the implications of this socialization process. Their interview responses often mirrored the mitigated conceptions of agency for their sentencing verdicts that were presented to them during trial.

TEXAS'S SENTENCING SCHEME, JURY INSTRUCTIONS, AND JUROR ACCOUNTABILITY

The special issue questions used in Texas capital trials present an ambiguous picture to jurors as to their individual roles in defendants' death sentences. The language of jurors' written sentencing instructions compounds this ambiguity, leaving jurors with conflicted and often confused ideas about their responsibility for defendants' sentences. The following texts, drawn from written jury instructions in one Texas case,[5] suggest that jurors are not the ultimate agents in sentencing defendants. Who, then, is responsible for sentencing? Most legal language, jury instructions included, cites either the "court" (the judge) or the circumstances of the crime itself as the primary agent in determining a defendants' sentence. These instructions accompany jurors in the deliberation room and serve as the only visibly codified guidance offered to them during their deliberations. The next three excerpts are drawn from one capital jury sentencing charge:[6]

> You have found the Defendant guilty of the offense of capital murder. As a result of that finding of guilt, and in order for *the Court to assess a proper punishment*, it is now necessary for *you to determine . . . the answers to certain questions.*

In this first text, "the Court," which serves as grammatical agent and subject of the action ("assess[ing] a proper punishment"),

---

5. In the cases which I observed, no pattern jury instructions were used. Rather, prosecutors and defense attorneys each presented drafts of proposed jury instructions and, based on these drafts, judges composed the final version.

6. Jurors receive separate charges for each stage of the trial—the guilt phase and sentencing phase.

is identified as the primary authority over a defendant's punishment. It is relevant to note that the judge—a person—is consistently referred to as the "Court"—a thing. This underscores the legal model that a death sentence is something that emerges from interpersonal institutional actions, rather than human decisions. Jurors' responsibility is then limited in this passage to determining "answers to certain questions." The causal chain represented here is that jurors find guilt and answer questions, after which the judge determines a punishment. Only later will the potential death of the defendant occur, which is not referenced explicitly.

In the next excerpt from jurors' punishment instructions, the "evidence" is positioned as agent of the sentencing decision, as it directs the jurors toward or against imposing the death penalty.

> *Evidence* of the background or character or the circumstances of the offense *that militates for or mitigates against the imposition of the death penalty . . .*

In this part of the instructions, the jurors' involvement in imposing death is attenuated in two ways. First, "the evidence" is construed as the responsible agent that "militates for" or "mitigates against" the death penalty. Second, the actual act of sentencing, "the imposition," is nominalized, which further eliminates a human agent from the action (Billig 2008; Ehrlich 2001, 39).

Further along in the charge, the jurors are reminded again that it is the court that actually imposes the sentence.

> You are instructed under the law applicable in this case, if *the jury answers* that a *circumstance or circumstances warrant* that a sentence of life imprisonment without the possibility of

> parole rather than a death sentence be imposed, *the Court will sentence the defendant* to imprisonment in the institutional division of the Texas Department of Criminal Justice for life without the possibility of parole.

In this excerpt, "the Court" is again represented as the agent of sentencing the defendant ("the court will sentence the defendant") and the jurors are relegated to answering the special issue questions ("the jury answers"). Their human agency is further mitigated in that "circumstances" [of the crime], rather than their decisions, are named as warranting the imposition of a particular sentence. This is consistent with findings stating that capital jurors often cite the crime committed as the primary justification for their sentence of death (Geimer and Amsterdam 1989).

After jurors have deliberated, signed their verdict forms, and re-entered the courtroom, the judge then pronounces a sentence on the defendant, during which he or she reiterates the formulations of agency within the jury charge. The following text is excerpted from one judge's address to the entire courtroom after the jury had finished their deliberations and handed in their verdict sheet:

C [READING ALOUD] : A *jury having answered* in the affirmative special issue number one, also having answered in the affirmative special issue number two, and having answered in the negative as to special issue number three,[7] *I assess your punishment* as death by lethal injection.

7. In Texas, if the defendant is charged as a party to a crime (i.e., multiple people were involved), jurors must answer a third special issue question.

In this proclamation, jurors are again positioned as responsible for answering the special issue questions, while the judge individually assesses the punishment. The ultimate authority for sentencing, as laid out by the Texas sentencing scheme and jurors' instructions, is thereby placed in the hands of the judge, not the individual jurors or the jury as a collectivity.

VOIR DIRE AS SOCIALIZATION INTO KILLING

The capital voir dire is unique in its extensive individual questioning of venire persons, which often takes longer than the trial itself. This stage of the trial includes the notorious "death qualification" process,[8] during which prospective jurors must "publicly affirm their willingness to take the most extreme legal action ever available to a juror" (Haney 1984, 143). If a venire person proclaims that he or she would not be willing to sentence the defendant to death, he or she is excused from the jury pool outright. In capital voir dires, moreover, jurors are presented with their sentencing guidelines upfront, even though they do not use them until the second phase of the trial. It has been extensively argued that this foregrounding of the special issue questions prejudices jurors unfairly toward giving the death penalty (Bowers 2003; Haney 1997).

Because of its extensive scope and probing content (Haney 1984, 149), the capital voir dire is the primary site for jurors' institutional transformations, in which linguistic constructions

---

8. See the 1984 special issue of *Law and Human Behavior* (vol. 8(1–2)) for a critical discussion of death qualification and its implications.

of agency play a crucial role. During jury selection, potential jurors are spoken to en masse by attorneys and judges, but are also, significantly, questioned individually by the same. This questioning is informed by extensive written questionnaires that venire persons fill out the first day they arrive for jury duty. Voir dire is the only time throughout a trial in which jurors can speak directly to court personnel, and attorneys and judges can speak relatively freely, as they are not bound by the laws of evidence. Through this intimate and relatively unconstrained process of questioning, attorneys and judges socialize jurors into particular, usually contrastive, models of how to serve on a capital jury and, more specifically, how to sentence a capital defendant. It thus proves an invaluable opportunity for attorneys to initiate and train jurors in their respective ways of seeing a case (cf. Goodwin 1994), specifically in how to characterize a juror's role in potentially taking the life of another person.

As a crucial element of jurors' socialization, attorneys and judges provide venire persons with linguistic frameworks through which the sentencing act becomes more conceivable, allowing jurors to confirm explicitly in voir dire that they could in fact sentence the defendant to death, which the death qualification process requires (Haney 1984, 140). As discussed in chapter 3, jurors are ultimately instructed that, once they take the oath to be a juror, their personal beliefs and feelings must be set aside in order to "follow the law." Through this process of confirmation, questions of life or death are converted into legal rules, ultimately eclipsing the reality of violence that lies beneath them. Certain people, however, concede from the beginning that they would not be able to sentence someone to death under any circumstances—they cannot "follow the law"—and are thereby ineligible to fill the role of capital juror.

During the jury empaneling I observed, one judge explained the process as follows: "They [venire persons] might be able to follow the law and they might not be able to. If they couldn't, we would have to dismiss them." The same judge later described the transformation jurors must undergo to the jury panel:

> So what we're saying is that everybody is free to disagree with these rules up until the time they become a juror and if they do have a disagreement, they must be able to set it aside. Your obligation is to follow and to enforce the rules that will be given in the court's charge.

The capital voir dire thus serves, in part, to select those venire persons who would be willing ultimately to sentence someone to death—to "put aside" their personal beliefs about the death penalty and follow the law. Capital jurors are thus instructed from the very beginning of trial that their sentencing decisions are not a product of their own, personal convictions, but are acts of "following" and "enforcing" the rules. This process has the consequence of, in many cases, stripping jurors' sentencing decisions of the individual, moral character (Weisberg 1983) that the post-*Furman* Supreme Court decisions require of them.

Attorneys' and judges' language during voir dire builds particular models for jurors regarding how they should think about their roles in sentencing a capital defendant.[9] The excerpts below are additional excerpts from judges' oral

9. As with jury charges, what Texas judges say to jurors during the voir dire is up to each individual judge, though there are some limitations as to what they may instruct the jury on (how consistently these are followed, however, is another question) and many of them loosely follow a general script.

directives to venire panels, and are quite representative of
the many judges I observed:

> One of those possible punishments is life and one of those
> possible punishments is death. Whatever *punishment is im-
> posed* will depend upon how *the jury answers three questions—*
> three special issues. . . . We talked about how *the jury answers
> those question[s] dictates what punishment I'm obligated to
> impose.*

> At the time you get to question 3, you will have done every
> single thing you can possibly do to *vote in such a way that I'm
> obligated to sentence the Defendant to death.*

As illustrated in these texts, the judge is portrayed as the agent
behind the punishment, while the jury is characterized as answering questions and voting in a way that will "dictate" a particular punishment from the judge. To jurors, as their interview
responses will show, this was often interpreted as meaning that
they are not primary agents in sentencing defendants to death.

In the following voir dire excerpt, another judge's address to the jury panel further explains the issue:

> If your jury answers yes to question number one and if your
> jury answers yes to question number two and if your jury an-
> swers no to question number three, the law says I have no
> choice. I have no option. I have no discretion. *I must sentence
> the Defendant to death . . . juries in the state of Texas do not go out
> and deliberate and subjectively determine, we'll give this defend-
> ant life in this case. We'll give that defendant death in that case.*
> Instead, what we do is we have juries make objective findings as
> to what the evidence is—your evaluation of that evidence—and
> *you use that evidence in answering each of these three questions.*
> Secondly, your verdict. While *you, the jury, do not yourselves*

sentence somebody to life or sentence somebody to death, you may answer these questions instead but you know the result of your answer. *Yes, yes and no in that order is a death.* Anything else is a life. The third thing is: your answers to these questions are not suggestions to me as to what sentence I should impose. They are not advisory to me. They are not recommendations to me as to what sentence I should impose. *Your answers to these questions direct me to impose* one sentence or the other.

This judge's monologue depicts a complicated network of persons responsible for differing elements of a sentencing decision. Consistent with the logic of jury charges, the juror's sole individual responsibility is to answer yes or no to the special issue questions,[10] not to impose a particular sentence.

The judge here tells jurors directly that they do not vote for life or death, for this kind of decision-making would be subjective and thus not up to legal standards, which in his words require "objective findings" based on the evidence. In terms of the judge's role, he explicitly states that he is the one to do the actual sentencing, though he disavows any choice in this action thus mitigating his *own* agency in the process ("the law says I have no choice. I have no option. I have no discretion"). The judge directly expresses jurors' attenuated responsibility for sentencing: "You, the jury, do not yourselves sentence somebody to life or sentence somebody to death." Despite the nature of this decision-making scheme, however, the judge asserts that jurors should realize the result of their decisions, which is a sentence of life or death ("you know the result of your answer").

10. This trial occurred before the elimination of the original 1st special issue question in the Texas sentencing scheme, which focused on the crime as a deliberate action. There were thus three special issue questions given in this case's sentencing charge.

If we approach this passage from the perspective of grammatical agency, we see an even more nuanced picture of the judge's complicated attributions of responsibility in sentencing decisions. Again consistent with the charge's language, the only context in which a juror is cited as an explicit agent of some act is in answering the special issue questions or in evaluating the evidence: "if *your jury answers yes* to question number one and if *your jury answers* yes to question number two and if *your jury answers* no to question number three," and "*juries make* objective findings." In references to the actual sentence of life or death, in contrast, the grammatical agent is not the jury, but the judge: "*I must sentence* the defendant to death," "*me to impose* one sentence or another."

The judge also depicts jurors' responsibility as a collective burden in this example, citing "your jury," rather than any individual juror, as agents in sentencing decisions. When the judge uses the second-person pronoun to addresses the jury, he specifies the addressee as the jury as a whole ("if *your jury* answers yes," "juries make objective findings," "*you, the jury*, do not yourselves sentence"). Referring to the jury's collective duty to answer questions potentially mitigates individual jurors' responsibility for defendants' fates.[11] These elements of the judge's instructions are indeed consistent with post-*Furman* requirements, which assert that "the jury," rather than individual jurors, must operate with awareness of its "awesome responsibility" (*Caldwell v. Mississippi* 1985).

---

11. For a thorough discussion of the relationship between collective agency and moral responsibility, see the 2006 special issue of *Midwest Studies in Philosophy*, 30(1).

When the judge explicitly connects jurors' answers to their life-or-death consequences, moreover, the agent is not the juror him- or herself, or even the jury as a whole, but the juror's *answer* to the special issue questions: "Yes, yes and no in that order is a death. Anything else is a life"; "*Your answers* to these questions *direct me* to impose one sentence or the other." This judge, in one of his first addresses to the jury panel, thus gave the jurors a complicated and potentially confusing picture of their (lack of) responsibility for the defendant's life or death sentence.

Many attorneys, not surprisingly, use the individual questioning of venire persons as a time to socialize jurors into ways of making sentencing decisions that will benefit their side of the case. Before their individual questioning of venire persons, attorneys scour the lengthy questionnaires the potential jurors filled out, and in most cases determine whether they think the venire person would tend toward a life or death verdict. The next excerpt is drawn from one prosecutor's individual questioning of a venire person. The prosecutor's summation of the decision-making process recapitulates the formulation of agency suggested in the written jury instructions above: the special issue framework keeps jurors free from the ultimate responsibility for sentencing a defendant.

> You feel a little more comfortable after the judge explained these issues and the process you go through. *It's not just a yes or no where you decide.* What you're doing is *you're basically answering the question.*

This structure, he explained, makes the decision easier on jurors. They do not have to "decide"; they merely have to answer the question. The same prosecutor later framed jurors' decisions similarly while questioning a different potential juror:

> Let me tell you how it works and see if you can sit on a jury
> that involves the potential assessment of the death penalty....
> *You don't write life or death. You answer certain questions* and
> you never get to those three questions unless you've already
> found the defendant guilty of capital murder.

Here, the prosecutor again assured the potential juror that his only duty is to answer special issue questions, not to sentence someone to death. He evokes the special issue framework written in the jury charge, assuring the prospective juror that he will not have to write in an answer of life or death when signing the form, but only answers to the special issue questions.

In direct contradiction to this prosecutor's explanatory framework, the defense attorney in the same case approached the issue in the following way:

> D: You know that *if you answer that question no*, there is
> no mitigation, *the defendant is going to get the death
> penalty from the judge.*
> J: That's right.
> D: Just as sure as *if you signed death on the line.*
> J: That's right.

In his reference to a hypothetical death sentence, this defense attorney acknowledged that the judge is the ultimate agent for giving the death penalty. But he highlighted the juror's responsibility in the process by transforming the verdict form from a list of special issue questions to one that might as well contain a signature line on which the juror must choose life or death. The defense attorney thus explicitly involved the juror in the execution of the defendant, in contrast to the judge's and prosecutor's configuration of agency in the earlier texts.

While questioning other venire persons, this same defense attorney made the life-and-death consequences of the juror's potential decision even more explicit:

> Let's assume a hypothetical situation. You got to the phase of the trial where *you would be considering whether someone lives or dies,* i.e., whether someone goes to prison for life or whether someone goes to prison to *await his execution.*

This defense attorney cut through the ambiguities of the judge's and prosecutor's language and portrayed the potential juror as the explicit agent of the defendant's death. The juror's role in the defendant's death is heightened by reference to the execution itself, which is ironically quite rare in capital trials (Sarat 2001).[12] Attorneys often used these alternative framings of jurors' responsibility for defendants' deaths in attempts to either keep or qualify venire persons for the jury. In the prosecutor's questioning above, for instance, the prosecutor wanted those particular individuals to serve on the jury. He thus mitigated their roles in defendants' deaths to ensure that those venire persons would be death qualified. Many potential jurors, in contrast, were disqualified when presented with the framing of agency illustrated above, after stating that they could not in fact hypothetically sentence someone to death.

---

12. This issue is discussed further in chapter 2.

QUESTIONING JURORS ABOUT THEIR RESPONSIBILITY

The previous sections outlined linguistic models to which jurors are introduced during voir dire regarding their agency in sentencing defendants. This section delves more deeply into the intricate process of socialization jurors undergo during capital voir dire, especially regarding death qualification. It closely analyzes brief excerpts from the individual questioning of two potential jurors in order to flesh out the linguistic means by which jurors, with their prior opinions in tow, are fashioned into the types of jurors who can sit on capital cases. The first of these is a venire person who, according to his questionnaire, believed strongly in the death penalty. While being questioned by the prosecutor, however, he admitted that imposing a death sentence himself would be extremely hard:

> I was thinking to myself *it would be awful hard to sentence somebody to death*. I would really have to think about everything.

Here, the juror, while not positioning himself as the direct agent of the act—using the infinitive instead (it would be awful hard *to sentence* . . .)—explicitly referred to the death sentence, a relatively rare linguistic choice for jurors. The prosecutor continued to question him about his ability to give death:

> P: It's a real serious decision. I agree with you completely. Do you think *that's something that you're capable of?*
> J: Yes. It would be hard but, you know, I feel *I could do it.*

p: You feel a little more comfortable after the judge explained these issues . . . *you're basically answering the
question.* Do you feel a little bit better about knowing that?

j: A little bit better. It's clear—you know, it cleared it
up. . . . I guess if—if—*how do I say it?—the conditions
warranted* the facts of the case—*if it cries out,* you
know, *for more justice* than life in the penitentiary, I
guess that would be the only thing that—I guess that
would be the—

p: That would be the basis for *it* for you?

j: Yes.

The prosecutor first asked whether this potential juror could
sentence someone to death ("Do you think that's something
you're capable of?"), to which the juror unhesitatingly answered yes. The juror then placed himself as agent and subject of the act—*I could do it,* using the pronoun "it" rather
than naming the sentence explicitly as he did previously. The
prosecutor reminded the juror, however, that he's "basically
answering the question," thus reformulating the act the juror
began the exchange with ("sentence[ing] somebody to
death") into the act of answering the special issue questions.

Following this reminder, the juror began to recast the
potential death sentence in line with the prosecutor's model.
In a suggestive metalinguistic move, he voiced his uncertainty about how to word his next utterance ("how do I say
it?"), thus marking the evolution his thinking was undergo-
ing. He then reiterated the legal framework of institutional
agency he was given from the judge and attorneys up to this
point: he cited "the conditions" of the case as warranting a
particular sentence. He further claimed that a death sentence

would be appropriate "if it [the crime, I assume] "cries out . . . for more justice." The agent carrying out the death sentence is thus transformed into a nonhuman entity imbued with human attributes. Through this subtle manipulation of language, the potential juror began his transformation; the death sentence is converted from an act of individual agency to an institutional, depersonalized act of interpreting and applying laws and facts.

This venire person was then put through a questioning sequence common to the voir dires I observed. The prosecutor asked him to look the defendant in the eye and, once his gaze was affixed to the defendant, the attorney asked whether the juror could handle being "personally" responsible for a decision that would give this very person the death penalty. He again promptly answered yes:

> P: Take a look at Mr. Jackson [the defendant] over here. Can you see him?
>
> J: Yes.
>
> P: Okay. What I'd like to know is whether or not you could *personally participate in a decision* where *these three questions are answered in such a way that he receive the death penalty*? Could you do that?
>
> J: Yes.

A different venire person who expressed much greater initial trepidation with potentially sentencing someone to death was put through a similar series of questions:

> P: Now, believing in it and participating in it, that's two different things. I want you to take a look at Mr. Jackson over here. Can you see him?
>
> J: Yes.

P: What I'd like to know is whether or not you feel like if the evidence was appropriate if *you could personally participate in a decision where these questions are answered in such a way that Judge Burdette ordered the death of the defendant?* Could you *personally participate* in that kind of process?

J: It would be hard but—

P: Yes, sir. I understand that . . . do you think that's something you could do?

J: No.

P: You don't think you could participate in that process—personally participate in that process?

J: No, I don't.

The attorneys' grammatical encodings of agency in the above questioning sequences contain a few subtle, but important, differences. In the case of the first, the act of sentencing is conveyed through a grammatically agentless construction: "personally participate in a decision where these three questions are answered in such a way that he receive the death penalty?" This linguistic framing puts the defendant himself in the subject position of the sentencing act, thereby eclipsing the juror's agency entirely. The juror, in this formulation, is relegated to participating in "a decision," while the defendant appears as the responsible party for his own death sentence. It is important to note that it is the special issue questions in particular that separate the decision from the penalty.

In the second, the same underlying question takes the following grammatical structure: "personally participate in a decision where these questions are answered in such a way that Judge Bateson ordered the death of the defendant?" In this formulation, the juror's hypothetical decision is linked directly to this specific judge sitting in the courtroom as agent and subject of "ordering" the death sentence. Notice, additionally, that the first formulation highlights the penalty ("the death penalty"), while the second is formulated as a death ("the death of the defendant"). The venire person in the last excerpt, when confronted with this agentive construction, did not acquiesce, acknowledging that he could not impose a death sentence and thus could not fill the role of capital juror. He was promptly excused per agreement by both sides. It is evident in these excerpts that attorneys' language choices often mirror their varying strategies during voir dire, though not necessarily consciously. When addressing the second potential juror, who had middling attitudes toward the death penalty and thus would not make a strong juror for the prosecution, the prosecutor formulated his questions in such a way that eventually led to this venire person's disqualification.

JURORS' POSTVERDICT FORMULATIONS OF RESPONSIBILITY

The effects of the linguistic socialization described above rose to the surface in jurors' postverdict interview responses. Given the linguistic models of agency jurors encountered throughout their trial experiences, it is not surprising that when reflecting on their death penalty decisions, they utilized a number of tactics to diminish personal responsibility for their decisions. In an analysis of post-*Furman* Supreme Court decisions on capital sentencing requirements, Abramson argues that despite the theoretical desire for death sentences to remain the "obligation and the authority" of the jury, the reality of the sentencing frameworks used ultimately "confuse[s] jurors into thinking their choices are more constrained than they in fact are" (2000, 120–121). As the following excerpts from jurors' posttrial interviews illustrate, the jurors with whom I spoke indeed tended to conceptualize their decisions as highly constrained and thus in the hands of some entity outside themselves.

In the following excerpt, drawn from one juror's posttrial interview, the juror struggled with identifying who the "ultimate authority" for capital sentencing decisions is:

> . . . whether we're the final authority or not. *I think the judge can overrule sentence guide*—excuse me, sentencing, at some point, but I think *the jury decides guilt or innocence,* and then at least *makes the recommendation for penalty.*

This juror identified his role clearly in the guilt/innocence decision through an agentive construction typical to English: the jury (as agent and subject) decides the guilt or innocence of the defendant (as object of this act of deciding). After some consternation (marked through the hedges "I think" and "at least"),[13] he concluded that he and his fellow jurors merely made a recommendation to the judge regarding sentencing, rather than being the "deciders." In reality, however, Texas judges have no discretion in this regard. A judge merely presents a jury's sentencing verdict to a defendant and has no power to overrule it.[14] The structure of the jury charge, however, makes this juror's interpretation possible, as it does not

---

13. Linguistic "hedges" refer to words or other discourse devices that lessen the impact of an utterance. See, e.g., Markkanen and Schroder 1997.

14. Alabama is the only state in which judges have routinely override jury life verdicts to impose death sentences. Bowers et al. (2006) found that in states that allow judge overrides, jurors are more likely to shirk responsibility for the defendant's punishment.

ask jurors to give the defendant a particular sentence. The judge connects the dots, so to speak, when pronouncing the sentence, stating the implications of the "special issue" answers once the verdict is read.

An additional marker of jurors' attenuated sense of responsibility for their sentencing decisions is that many of the jurors I interviewed cited an abstract or nonhuman agent as controlling the sentencing process. This corresponds with Haney, Sontag, and Costanzo's findings that capital jurors in multiple states tend to abdicate responsibility for their decisions to the "law," the judge, or their instructions, ultimately evading the "life and death consequences" of their verdicts (1994, 160). The juror quoted below explained to me during an interview how he justified his decision to sentence the defendant to death:

> I determined going into this that I was going to do exactly *what the state asked me to do.* At the end of the day, that would be the only way I would feel good about it. . . . *Whatever the state asks, I'm going to rigidly abide by it.*

This juror emphatically bestowed the responsibility for his sentencing decision on "the state," a nonhuman, institutional representation of the criminal laws of Texas.

Many others jurors followed similar logic in talking about their decisions, citing other abstract entities, such as the law or a generalized and impersonal "they," as the responsible agents for sentencing. This practice is common in English, in which subjects and agents are constructed as nonanimate entities; this grammatical option allows an event that probably involved human agency to be framed as if it did not (Duranti 2004, 64). The jurors I interviewed often spent considerable time justifying and explaining their sentencing decisions to me. These explanations often involved similar constructions of agency, in which they cited nonhuman, often abstract agents as the impetus for their sentencing verdicts. The following excerpts, drawn from three separate juror interviews, illustrate this phenomenon:

JUROR 1: But it's not a, deciding that isn't a judgment based on what I feel. It's based on what *the charge* says. It's based on *the law.*

JUROR 2: *They* don't want someone who is not a continuing threat *to be put to death.*

JUROR 3: Make a good decision, *not for yourself,* not for—*for what the state of Texas is asking you to do,* and *they're* not asking you to put him to death. *They're* asking you to be very careful about what you decide.

Juror 1 attributes his decision to what the "charge" and the "law" dictate. He is willing to put aside his own feelings in order to honor this authority, as jurors must attest that they can do in order to be death qualified during voir dire. Juror 2 cites a generic "they," understood perhaps as the state, or the lawyers, or some other manifestations of legal authority, as wanting something from jurors in regards to sentencing. He then references the death sentence in an infinitive clause—to be put to death—which elides an agent entirely. Juror 3 frames his decision in terms again of what "they" want from the jurors, identified here specifically as the state of Texas.

A rather cynical juror—one more critical of the justice system than others I spoke to—explicitly contemplated the role of a jury in sentencing capital defendants. This juror, ironically, conceptualizes the jury as agents of the state in the legal sense: it is the jurors' role to take the moral and emotional onus off the state and carry out the death penalty on its behalf. If the state desires the death penalty, the jury serves as a buffer of sorts between representatives of the state and the defendants they kill:

> The jury's there to give the prosecutors, the judge, and the state a free ride. Because a man—if somebody's convicted of capital murder, I mean they're accused of it, they can confess to it. But *if the state wants to give him the death penalty, a judge can't do that. It's got to be the jury. . . .* It falls back on the twelve people. I mean, to me that's, uh, why we're there. To give everybody else a clean conscience.

PASSIVE CONSTRUCTIONS AND MITIGATED AGENCY

As modeled in their instructions, jurors also routinely abdicated responsibility for sentencing decisions by using the passive voice. This grammatical option allows an event to be described as if no agent, human or otherwise, is responsible for carrying out the action, which has been argued to mitigate the doer's responsibility for the action (Bohner 2001; Henley, Miller, and Beazley 1995). As evidenced in the following excerpts, jurors used these constructions when discussing why they felt confident in their sentencing verdicts:

JUROR 1 I felt comfortable with *the decision that had to be made* and *that was made.*

JUROR 2 We were all there six weeks. We were all there hearing the same thing . . . looking pictures at the same thing, and *the verdict came out this way.*

JUROR 3 My views of the death penalty are still the same. Um
because I think in this case *it was warranted.*

As opposed to recounting their sentencing decisions as
something they were personally involved in, jurors in these
examples removed agents entirely through the use of the passive voice. Instead of a juror making the decision in the first
excerpt, for instance, the decision "was made." By whom or
what is left unsaid. In addition to mitigating their own agency
in sentencing defendants through the passive voice, these
jurors, in a typical move, avoided speaking directly of death
sentences or executions. Instead, they referred to their "verdicts" or "the decision."

JUROR POLLING

Jurors' reluctance to admit individual responsibility for sentencing decisions was also evident in their hesitation to being
polled at the reading of verdicts. In capital cases, an attorney
may request that the jurors be individually polled in front of
the defendant and gallery when a verdict is read. Defense attorneys often requested polling for sentencing decisions on
the assumption that jurors who are on the fence about giving
life or death may be compelled to give life when faced with
the task of having to state their decision in front of the defendant, his family, and the trial audience. Jury polling runs
counter to the predominant theory of sentencing decisions
presented to jurors throughout the trial—that they only
answer special issue questions, judges are the primary agents
in sentencing, and jurors' decisions are collective. After being
inculcated to think of their decisions as acts for which they

share only partial responsibility, upon polling, jurors are forced to face, in front of an audience no less, the individual nature of their verdicts.

When requesting jury polling, attorneys are indeed picking up on a common attitude among capital jurors. Several of those I spoke with discussed their discomfort with this practice, as in the following examples from two jurors' interviews:

> But I know a lot of people would've been, not a lot, but there's two or three that would've been very much happier to just secret-ballot the whole thing and never be polled or anything else.

> It's hard then, you know, and, there again I think some of the females had it, felt it, the biggest burden, from that. Now some of them, boy, they wouldn't even question, you know. They didn't mind standing up and saying it. But others of them, other of them didn't mind voting for it, but it (may have) been uncomfortable to say it out loud.

Both jurors depicted particular fellow jurors as hesitant to be polled individually. The juror in the first excerpt argued against using a secret ballot in the jury room, reminding his fellow jurors that they would most likely have to proclaim their votes "out loud" at the reading of the verdict anyway. Both juries, however, did vote for death in the end, despite some jurors' trepidation.

COLLECTIVE AGENCY

The analysis of voir dire language above demonstrates that judges and attorneys often address the jury as a whole, rather than as individual jurors, when instructing them on their sentencing verdicts. Linguistic constructions of agency within jurors' interviews reflected this sense of collective responsibility. Lynch and Haney argue that the "subjectivity" of a capital sentencing decision makes it especially susceptible to group influence (2009, 483; cf. Kerr, Niedermeier, and Kaplan 1999).[15] The degree to which Supreme Court decisions and statutory law require jurors to take individual responsibility for their decisions about defendants' lives is unclear. The requirement that death decisions be rendered by juries stems from the desire that a punishment reflect the "community's sense of the defendant's 'moral guilt'" (Justice John Paul Stevens, cited in Sarat 1995, 1103). Jurors' sentencing decisions are thus collective in two senses: in their supposed representation of community values and the required unanimity among all jurors for a capital sentencing verdict.

Jurors' linguistic formulations when talking about the death penalty mark the collective character of their decisions; they often assign the agentive role to the jury as a whole, either referenced by "we," the generalized "you," or some other descriptor. The following interview excerpts from multiple jurors illustrate this phenomenon:

> I still think *we* should have given him the death penalty.

> *We're* going to be deciding on something, you know, life or death.

> Before *we decide* on this, giving him, what is it, the *death penalty* . . .

In these cases, the decision for death is depicted in explicit forms (e.g., "make a decision" vs. "give him the death penalty").

---

15. Research has shown that deliberation specifically guides juries in the direction of death verdicts (Lynch and Haney 2009; Bowers, Steiner, and Sandys 2001).

Jurors, as mentioned above, often avoided talking about the death penalty explicitly, referring more obliquely to their "decisions" or "verdicts." It is especially significant, therefore, that in these explicit mentions of the death penalty, jurors did not cite individual responsibility for sentencing defendants to death. Juries as collectivities are instead placed in the agent role in descriptions of these actions, thus mitigating jurors' individual roles in the sentencing decisions.

When part of a group, individual members are provided with a sense of anonymity (Grossman 2009, 149, 151), thus diminishing individual responsibility for actions. Jurors' desire to remain relatively anonymous with regard to their decisions was evident in multiple ways in my data. First was the general reluctance jurors felt to talk to me about their trial experiences, even among those who I ended up interviewing. One juror recounted the anger she felt when she received my letter asking her to participate in an interview. This same juror also expressed unease with the fact that attendees of the trial, including the victim's family, would see her around town and visually monitor her during the trial. I asked her the extent to which she thought about the trial after its end:

> I think for the most part I've done that. Just put it away. You know, as, when I got your letter, actually I was, um, came in and I threw it at my boyfriend, and I said, how did she get this information? He's like, I go, this is supposed to be over! And he's like [juror name] you don't have to call her. I'm like no, I'll talk to her, but after this it's done! And he's like okay. He's like but really, you don't have to talk to her, and I said okay.

This was a common response to my requests for interviews. Though their names were part of public record, jurors often revealed a desire to remain anonymous. Jurors' hesitation to be polled at the reading of the verdict displays this desire for anonymity as well.

Defense attorneys often attempted to combat the tendency for jurors to collectivize their responsibility for sentencing. Throughout trials, from the voir dire to sentencing closing statements, a primary tactic for defense attorneys was to continually submit to jurors that they are individual decision-makers. By emphasizing that jurors have their own individual vote, the attorneys hoped to convince hold out jurors for life to stay their ground and not fold to other "death" jurors. The following exchange, drawn from the individual voir dire questioning of a potential juror by a defense attorney, is typical of this tactic:

> J: I would vote, you know, my own feelings.
>
> D: Okay. And that's really important because as you look out into that jury box, you don't see a bench there. You see twelve individual seats. Would you agree with me?
>
> J: Right.
>
> D: . . . there are twelve judges and they are individuals, and a person on trial is entitled to rely on the *individual assessment* of *that individual juror*.

Despite attorneys emphasizing that a sentencing decision is to be individually assessed,[16] many jurors, as has been

---

16. Some states, such as Maryland, have added clauses to their juror sentencing instructions that add a third answer to the mitigation question in order to allow for individual jurors' opinions to be recognized. Instead of answering yes or no, they may also choose the option that states that the jurors could not come to a unanimous decision. The result of this choice would be a life sentence (*Mills v. Maryland*, 486 US 367, 1988).

reported in other studies of death penalty juries (Eisenberg and Wells 1993; Luginbuhl and Howe 1995), reported feeling pressured to come to a unanimous decision and thus did not hold out in defense of their own individual opinions. This raises the question as to whether post-*Furman* Supreme Court decisions require—and whether they *should* require—jurors to accept *individual* responsibility for their sentencing decisions. Given the unanimity requirement of capital sentencing verdicts and the ideological notion of juries as representatives of community values, it may be counterintuitive for many jurors to think of their decisions as truly individual acts. The finality and severe consequences of their decisions, however, arguably warrant that their assessments be carefully and individually determined.

FROM VIOLENCE TO RULES

In sum, these data reveal that few jurors in my study explicitly and unequivocally asserted their individual roles in decisions for death. In both trial talk and postverdict interviews, jurors—following the linguistic lead of prosecutors and judges—distanced themselves from their decisions for death through particular linguistic tactics.

Trial language, including written jury instructions, attorneys' questioning of jurors and judges' oral statements to jurors, conveyed contradictory guidelines as to how jurors should conceptualize their own responsibility for death sentences. During voir dire, prosecutors and defense attorneys socialize jurors into how to conceptualize their decisions. They attempt, according to their respective trial agendas, to convince jurors of their relative responsibility for their decisions. In many ways, these models of legal language urge jurors to treat death sentences as ultimately in the hands of someone or something else. Imbuing oneself or another with agency opens a person to moral evaluation (Duranti 2011). I suggest that even these subtle linguistic manipulations of responsibility give jurors the moral leeway needed in order to sentence another human being to death.

As the linguistic constructions above reveal, jurors are indeed led to believe—by their written and oral instructions and attorneys' talk during trial—that responsibility for the defendants' deaths "rests elsewhere" and sometimes, as made possible through particular grammatical constructions, in no human agent whatsoever. I argue, furthermore, that the very structure of Texas's sentencing procedure with its "special issue" framework exacerbates jurors' ability to shirk responsibility for their sentences (cf. Vartkessian, Sorensen, and Kelly 2014). Jurors, as their interview responses reveal, routinely expressed that they were not individually responsible for sentencing defendants to death.

I return now to a concern expressed at the beginning of this book and revisited in this chapter. As critics of the death penalty assert (Sarat 1995; Weisberg 1983), the capital trial process sanitizes the violence behind state killing, reducing it to a manipulation of legal rules. This purges references to the act of killing almost entirely from the process of death sentencing. When capital jurors are socialized into death penalty trials, they adopt linguistic models, based on attorneys', judges', and written legal language, that represent this process of reduction. Differing formulations of agency, more specifically, reveal legal models of responsibility that transform jurors from individual moral agents to participants in a rule-governed process that eventually leads to an execution.

The linguistic work presented in this chapter, which mitigates jurors' individual agency in death sentences, contrasts sharply with how jurors talk about defendants' agency in criminal acts of killing, which they regard as individual and intentional. The latter aligns with criminal requirements for culpability and informs how jurors think about punishment. One juror's postverdict response encapsulates this view: "You intentionally kill. I think you deserve to die, you know." Debates about the permissibility of the death penalty in the United States often circle around distinctions between jurors' and defendants' roles in acts of killing. Some claim that state killing is akin to murder; others contend that state-sanctioned executions and killings outside of the law are qualitatively different acts. According to many of the jurors with whom I spoke, they indeed conceptualized killing in these two contexts as incommensurable.

It has been argued that capital sentencing structures used throughout the United States obfuscate the real nature of jurors' decisions (Haney, Sontag, and Costanzo 1994). The communicative practices described above indeed provide jurors with potential emotional "shields" (Haney, Sontag, and Costanzo 1994, 172) from the life-and-death consequences of their decisions. The constructions of agency illustrated here, moreover, are part of the interactional machinery by which "ordinary citizens," according to Sarat, are enlisted as "authorizing agents for the law's own lethal brand of violence" (1995, 1103). Significantly, in the examples explored above, the mitigation of jurors' individual moral agency seems necessary for them to qualify to sit on a capital jury. Socializing jurors into their institutional roles (Eisenberg, Garvey, and Wells 1996) allows jurors to, as Cover argues, "act violently without experiencing . . . the normal degree of inhibition" (1986, 221) that would regulate the behavior of autonomous individuals. The democratic administration of the death penalty would thereby appear to necessitate the process of socialization described here, in its rendering of state killing a "kind of violence which," in Sarat's words again, "can be approved and rationally dispensed" (Sarat 1995, 41).

This chapter aimed to illuminate some of the specific communicative means by which cultural inhibitions against harming others can be transformed, on both an individual and societal level, into "cultural support" for violent acts (Sarat 1995, 1104). Such a transformation is made possible through the linguistic rationalization of violence. The ways in which state violence in the United States is legitimated and justified on a broader scale is revealed in the minutiae of interactions that constitute jurors' involvement with the death penalty system.

IMPLICATIONS FOR LEGAL PRACTICE

The analyses offered in this chapter have specific ramifications for capital counsel.[17] For one, empirical evidence shows that the structure of, or particular statements made during, a capital trial—for example, the special issues that statutes require the jury to answer, judges' and prosecutors' in-court characterizations of the jury's role, and the sentencing instructions given to the jury to guide deliberations—create an unacceptable likelihood that the jury will not feel responsibility for determining the appropriateness of a

---

17. I am indebted to John Niland and Jared Tyler for their input on this section.

death sentence. This reality may give rise to a claim under the Eighth Amendment.

The data also reveal that jurors who should not be qualified to sit in a death case are in fact chosen as death penalty jurors, specifically those who cannot take responsibility for defendants' sentences. Counsel should be familiar with techniques (1) for exposing those prospective jurors who would automatically impose the death penalty following a murder conviction or finding that the defendant is death eligible, regardless of the individual circumstances of the case and (2) for rehabilitating potential jurors whose initial indications of opposition to the death penalty make them possibly excludable. This study suggests that more attention should be paid during death qualification to the degree to which venire persons will be able to give adequate weight to their "awesome responsibility" when sentencing. Defense attorneys should also be aware of potentially damaging and objectionable directives to jurors from judges and prosecutors.

My research demonstrates further that jury instructions (whether oral or written) are often contradictory, confusing, and in violation of constitutional law. Trial counsel should request jury instructions and verdict forms that ensure that jurors will be able to consider and give effect to all relevant mitigation evidence and that direct jurors to take personal responsibility for defendants' sentences. Trial counsel should object to instructions or verdict forms that are constitutionally flawed, inaccurate, or confusing and should offer alternative instructions.

7

Conclusion: Linguistic Dehumanization and Democracy

THE DEATH PENALTY IS ONE of those things that may seem just and appropriate in the abstract, but once you are privy to the minutia of its production, it becomes much less appealing. Those who encounter the American system of capital punishment—jurors, attorneys, defendants—though they may initially support it unquestioningly, are often left disillusioned and frustrated and eventually come to oppose it. During my research, I spoke to a former prison warden who oversaw years of executions at Walls. He has since publicly denounced the death penalty, admitting during our interview that he hated "messin'" with executions. A juror with whom I spoke also described his change of heart regarding capital punishment after his service:

> J: I've always felt that the death penalty, you know, was a good thing. This process here is kind of, makes you want to, makes me want to think about it.
>
> R: How so?

J: . . . It's like I say, that's the hardest thing I ever had to do. And I never thought that it would be that hard. That's w—I don't know how to word it. It's [exhale] it was just hard and . . . I think if somebody gets life in prison, that ought to mean what it means.

As they become ever more aware of botched executions and innocent defendants nearly escaping their extermination, people across the nation are losing trust in capital punishment, just as this warden and this juror have. But while an increasing number of citizens become averse to the death penalty in the United States inside and outside of Texas, the machinery of death[1] continues to operate.

The fundamental gears and cogs that maintain its continual motion are composed largely of language. It is the words with which attorneys address potential jurors during voir dire, the written instructions on which jurors rely in the deliberation room, and the talk about defendants throughout trial that maintain the persistent operation of the death penalty. By subverting other forms of experience, moreover, particular, authoritative modes of language allow jurors to send defendants to their deaths.

LEGAL LANGUAGE, DEHUMANIZATION, AND DEMOCRACY

A central argument of this book has been that the language of death penalty trials constitutes acts of discursive violence, which deny the full consideration of defendants' humanity as

---

1. This phrase is taken from Supreme Court Justice Blackmun's now famous dissent in *Callins v. Collins* (510 U.S. 1141, 1994), in which he avows to no longer "tinker with the machinery of death."

required (though dubiously enforced) by death penalty law. Theories of discursive violence, especially in relation to law, often speak of linguistic acts used with the intent to harm others (Corsevski 1998; for an exception, see MacKinnon 1993). This book has revealed that Texas death penalty jurors, lawyers, and judges engage in more subtle, often unintentional acts of discursive violence that are embedded in the legal system itself. The violence within the US criminal justice system is therefore not limited to overt acts of bodily harm, but is "inextricably linked to the problem of representation" (Coates and Wade 2007, 511). Specifically, death penalty trials entail a variety of communicative distancing practices—talk of facts and evidence that eclipse embodied encounters during trial, dehumanizing references to defendants that stymie empathy between them and jurors, written and oral instructions that allow jurors to deny their personal involvement in defendants' deaths—that deny the humanistic side of legal decision-making.

An additional goal of this book has been to use the language of death penalty trials as a window into the American legal system more broadly. The practices of discursive violence upon which capital punishment relies are embedded within ideologies of objectivity, neutrality, and the rule of law that are integral to the US legal system (Comaroff and Comaroff 2004; Krause 2011). According to these related principles, reason and objectivity should triumph over the mercurial swings of individual feelings and opinions to achieve impartiality; law and reason thus become paired to the exclusion of other forms of human understanding. This exclusion is ensured in part by authoritative legal discourses about, for instance, evidence and facts.

In practice, these discourses lead jurors and others engaged in doing law to put aside human elements of legal decision-making in the name of objectivity. Jurors' acts of linguistic distancing in capital trials are justified by—if not, from the jurors' perspectives, required by—authoritative legal language, such as jury charges and judges' words. These distancing acts, importantly, are built into the system of law itself. Democratic regimes and the institutions that support them in fact rely on the management of power through language (Coates and Wade 2007; Fairclough 1989; Foucault 1984). Dominant ideologies within these regimes are actualized through the face-to-face interaction of individuals within these institutions (Coates and Wade 2007, 511). The US legal system thus operates in part through the careful management of the experiential phenomena that make up legal practice.

The point that many legal scholars and practitioners miss is that these ideologies of rationality, objectivity, and impartiality, upon which our legal system rests, are culturally specific. They have come to undergird the practice of American law through historically and socially specific events and circumstances (Tamanaha 2004). What gets lost when we forget (or erase) the *relative* value of these ideologies is what potentially harmful practices and ideas they promote. In the American case, ideologies of rationality and objectivity dominate a legal system reliant on evidence-based decisions and the ideal of jurors as fact-finders. This is a system that restricts embodied and empathic experiences, thus encouraging dehumanizing acts of discursive violence.

JURIES, DEHUMANIZATION, AND DEMOCRACY

In the case of Texas death penalty trials, probing into jurors' words reveals a potentially contradictory and somewhat surprising picture of what many have lauded as the bulwark of democracy: the jury. Historical accounts of the development of the jury trial tout its central role in the development and legitimation of democratic governance (e.g., McClanahan 2009; Vidmar and Hans 2007; 1986; Forsyth 1878). Stories of the American jury track its origin to a desire to allow a human, community-based element in legal decision-making, thus protecting the individual from arbitrary governmental power (McClanahan 2009; Appleman 2009). The jury is thus often represented as the archetypical democratic institution, given its representative and participatory character; "the will of the jury is equated to that of the community" (Chibundu 2006, 6).

Juries in practice, however, operate according to a potentially incongruous goal. While the jury's democratic character rests in part on its metonymic representation of community perspectives, its value is also seen to rest in its promotion of impartial, unbiased decision-making. My research on jury decision-making in American death penalty trials has found, in fact, that capital jurors tend to eschew this first democratic value of the jury—its promotion of community-based, empathetic understanding of defendants (cf. Appleman 2009; Chibundu 1999)—in the name of the other, contradictory one—its design as an impartial, objective legal body (Landsman 2002). Thus, while the idea of the jury is that it evokes sympathy for defendants by calling upon their "peers"—individuals who are socially and geographically "close"—to judge them (*Strauder v. West Virginia*, 100 U.S. 303 (1980)), American jurors may in fact employ contradictory images of an ideal juror to create distance between themselves and defendants, ultimately dehumanizing them.

In an attempt to legitimize burgeoning democratic regimes, nations across the globe are increasingly adopting lay judging institutions (Sheyn 2010). These movements, however, take for granted that certain democratic values, such as increasing the human component of legal practice and imperviousness to individual corruption, are in fact promoted by the use of jury trials. The jury is still out, as it were, on many of these international adaptations of lay judging. The findings from this book regarding the contradictions embedded in jury practice thus have significant implications for contexts in which jury trials are adopted in an effort to stimulate more humanistic legal systems.

SOME WORDS FOR LEGAL PRACTITIONERS

Within critical legal scholarship, there has been a significant push to "rehumanize law,"[2] given that "the dry and disconnected discourse of legal authorization" limits the "full range of human elements" in legal decision-making (Haney 1997, 1485). As Justice Brennan of the Supreme Court has argued, the language of judging must be expanded to reflect the "subjective, experiential, and emotional" influences of decision-making (Henderson 1988, 123; Nussbaum 1996) in order to achieve just verdicts.

But many fear opening the legal system to such purportedly unreliable and damaging additions. Susan Bandes, as discussed earlier, recognizes the danger in allowing experiential

---

2. Literary legal scholarship, such as Gordon's (2011) recent book from whose title I borrowed this phrase, suggests that narrative is the appropriate vehicle through which such rehumanization can be realized. This book assumes that that all of law is narrative in nature, including the dehumanizing narratives that are at the base of the critique.

phenomena such as empathy into legal processes without "sufficient structural safeguards," as they could invite arbitrariness into the system (1996, 399). The question remains, how can the US legal system respond to such humanistic critiques in practice? Will such a response necessarily harm the legal system rather than help it?

My suggested answers to these questions range from minute and concrete to more foundational considerations. This book has identified a number of specific uses of language that lead to the dehumanization of defendants by not permitting jurors to consider their individuality in full as required by the Supreme Court. This is enabled in large part by Texas's penalty phase instructions and sentencing schema. While it has been argued elsewhere that jurors misunderstand their instructions in capital trials to mean that death sentences are required upon findings of guilt (Bowers 2003; Haney 1997; Miller and Hayward 2008), this book points to specific linguistic constructions—such as clauses regarding emotion and grammatical encodings of agency—that result in these misunderstandings of jurors' duties. The language of capital sentencing charges in Texas should therefore be revised to clarify (1) the meaning of jurors' individual, moral judgments and what forms of information—including their own and others' emotional and embodied experiences—they should be allowed to consider and (2) jurors' personal role in and responsibility for defendants' sentences and subsequent deaths.

In addition, the capital voir dire needs to be subject to much greater scrutiny, especially given the fact that it occupies such a consequential position within capital trials. The death qualification process has been criticized for composing juries that are death prone from the start (Bowers 2003; Dillehay and Sandys 1996; Haney 1997). Capital voir dire does demonstrably more than this, however, that places the constitutionality of death penalty juries in question. The language judges and attorneys use both in jury empaneling and in individual questioning socializes jurors into the dehumanizing practices outlined above, thereby creating juries that are prone to disregard concerns about the individual lives of defendants.

On a more generalized level, the analyses within this book encourage a rethinking—by legal scholars and practitioners alike—of what constitutes language. The first step is to dissolve the harsh distinctions between language and emotion, mind and body, and reason and empathy that are entailed in legal language and treat them as integrated phenomena dialogically constructed through human interaction. By teaching legal actors to see language in an unfamiliar way, language and law scholars can help mitigate dehumanizing effects of legal practice. This includes investigating how legal experiences are shaped or elided and the consequences this has for justice. Those searching to humanize our legal system will therefore benefit from a more complete understanding of how language as experience operates in law and how specific legal discourses lead jurors to curtail certain experiential phenomena. Legal critics who wish to eradicate the subjective elements of legal decision-making fear the *uncertainty* of human experience; but its *expulsion* is the real danger to just legal practice.

HUMANIZING LAW

This book has revealed that capital jurors must navigate a central tension between (1) legal language and ideologies that conceal defendants' humanity and (2) humanizing encounters with defendants copresent in the courtroom. More generally, the book has demonstrated how language plays a key role in the making and unmaking of defendants into human beings. As a result of the language practices analyzed in the preceding chapters, the lives and humanity of defendants are called into question well before the literal taking of life occurs.

Legal contexts amplify the world-making function of language, as they constitute realms in which judges and jurors make practically consequential decisions about other people's lives. Cover (1986) places this attribute of legal language at the center of what he argues to be law's necessary violence. The preceding analyses have indeed shown that transforming a human being into a particular institutional person—a defendant—facilitates jurors' making decisions to take his life.

Jurors' reflections have revealed, however, that despite the power inherent in legal language, the primordial human encounter—the ethical relationship to the other as embodied in the face (Levinas 1985; 1969)—is never fully institutionally suppressed. In his haunting memoir about serving as an execution warden, Donald Cabana writes of his relationship with a particular death row inmate. The following passage vividly depicts the human encounter that many jurors struggle with during death penalty trials:

> Connie Ray Evans and I transcended our environment and the roles in which we had been cast. The two of us had somehow managed to become real people to each other. There were no more titles or social barriers behind which either of us could hide. I was no longer a prison warden, and he had become someone other than a condemned prisoner. We were just two

ordinary human beings caught up in a vortex of events that neither of us could control. (Cabana 1998, 16–17)

In capital trials, as in this warden's relationship with a man on death row, jurors deal with both the institutional, dehumanizing discourse of the law and the vulnerability of face-to-face encounters, which may give them pause about sending a man to his death. It is in the intricate, embodied communicative interactions of capital trials that the workings of this particular form of state violence are negotiated. On a practical level, while capital punishment remains a legal reality, lessons from this book provide insight into ways to curtail its implementation.

BIBLIOGRAPHY

Abramson, Jeffrey. 2000. *We, the Jury: The Jury System and the Ideal of Democracy*. Cambridge, MA: Harvard University Press.

Adler, Robert S., and Ellen R. Peirce. 1993. "The Legal, Ethical, and Social Implications of the 'Reasonable Woman' Standard in Sexual Harassment Cases." *Fordham Law Review* 61, no. 4: 773–827.

Agamben, Giorgio. 1995. *Homo Sacer: Sovereign Power and Bare Life*. Translated by Daniel Heller-Roazen. Stanford, CA: Stanford University Press.

Agar, Michael H. 1980. *The Professional Stranger: An Informal Introduction to Ethnography*. New York: Academic Press.

Ahearn, Laura. "Agency." *Journal of Linguistic Anthropology* 9 (1999): 9–12.

Ahearn, Laura. 2001. "Language and Agency." *Annual Review of Anthropology* 30: 109–137.

Ahearn, Laura. 2011. *Living Language: An Introduction to Linguistic Anthropology*. Malden, MA: Wiley-Blackwell.

Amsterdam, Anthony G., and Jerome Bruner. 2009. *Minding the Law*. Cambridge, MA: Harvard University Press.

Appleman, Laura I. 2009. "The Lost Meaning of the Jury Trial Right." *Indiana Law Journal* 84: 397–446.

Associated Press. 2014. "Three Executions Gone Wrong: Details of Lethal Injections in Arizona, Ohio, Oklahoma." *San Jose Mercury News*. July 24. http://www.mercurynews.com/crime-courts/

ci_26208588/three-executions-gone-wrong-details-lethal-injections-arizona.

Austin, John L. 1962. *How to Do Things with Words: The William James Lectures Delivered at Harvard University in 1955.* Oxford: Clarendon Press.

Badzinski, Diane M., and Ann Burnett Pettus. 1994. "Nonverbal Involvement and Sex: Effects on Jury Decision Making." *Journal of Applied Communication Research* 22, no. 4: 309–321.

Baker, C. L. 1995. "Contrast, Discourse Prominence, and Intensification, with Special Reference to Locally Free Reflexives in British English." *Language* 71: 63–101.

Baker, Katherine K. 2005. "Gender and Emotion in Criminal Law." *Harvard Journal of Law and Gender* 28: 447–466.

Balch, Robert W., Curt T. Griffiths, Edwin L. Hall, and L. Thomas Winfree. 1976. "Socialization of Jurors: The Voir Dire as a Rite of Passage." *Journal of Criminal Justice* 4, no. 4: 271–283.

Bandes, Susan. 1996. "Empathy, Narrative, and Victim Impact Statements." *University of Chicago Law Review* 63, no. 2: 361–412.

Bandes, Susan. 1999. "Introduction." In *The Passions of Law*, edited by Susan Bandes. New York: New York University Press, 1–15.

Bandes, Susan. 2008a. "Child Rape, Moral Outrage, and the Death Penalty." *Northwestern University Law Review Colloquy* 103: 17–28.

Bandes, Susan. 2008b. "Framing Wrongful Convictions." *Utah Law Review* 5: 5–24.

Barnett, Mark A., Pat A. Tetreault, Jody A. Esper, and Ann R. Bristow. 1986. "Similarity and Empathy: The Experience of Rape." *Journal of Social Psychology* 126, no. 1: 47–49.

Barron, David. 2003. "I Did Not Want to Kill Him but Thought I Had To." *Journal of Law and Policy* 11, no. 1: 207–254.

Bauman, Richard, and Charles L. Briggs. 2003. *Voices of Modernity: Language Ideologies and the Politics of Inequality.* New York: Cambridge University Press.

Benforado, Adam. 2010. "The Body of the Mind: Embodied Cognition, Law, and Justice." *St. Louis University Law Journal* 54: 1–32

Bentele, Ursula, and William J. Bowers. 2001. "How Jurors Decide on Death: Guilt Is Overwhelming; Aggravation Requires Death; and Mitigation Is No Excuse." *Brooklyn Law Review* 66: 1011–1080.

Bernard, H. 2006. Russell. *Research Methods in Anthropology: Qualitative and Quantitative Approaches*. 4th ed. Walnut Creek, CA: Altamira Press.

Besteman, Catherine Lowe. 1999. *Unraveling Somalia: Race, Violence, and the Legacy of Slavery*. Philadelphia: University of Pennsylvania Press.

Billig, Michael. 2008. "The Language of Critical Discourse Analysis: The Case of Nominalization." *Discourse and Society* 19, no. 6: 783–800.

Bohner, G. 2001. "Writing about Rape: Use of the Passive Voice and Other Distancing Text Features as an Expression of Perceived Responsibility of the Victim." *British Journal of Social Psychology* 40: 515–529.

Bourdieu, Pierre. 1977. *Outline of a Theory of Practice*. Translated by Richard Nice. Cambridge: Cambridge University Press.

Bourdieu, Pierre. 1979. "Symbolic Power." *Critique of Anthropology* 4: 77–85.

Bourdieu, Pierre. 1990. *The Logic of Practice*. Translated by Richard Nice. Stanford, CA: Stanford University Press.

Bowers, William J. 1995. "The Capital Jury Project: Rationale, Design, and Preview of Early Findings." *Indiana Law Journal* 70, no. 4: 1043–1102.

Bowers, William J. 2003. "Still Singularly Agonizing: Laws Failure to Purge Arbitrariness from Capital Sentencing." *Criminal Law Bulletin* 39: 51–86.

Bowers, William J., Benjamin D. Fleury-Steiner, and Michael E. Antonio. 2003. "The Capital Sentencing Decision: Guided Discretion, Reasoned Moral Judgment, or Legal Fiction." In *America's Experiment with Capital Punishment: Reflections on the Past, Present, and Future of the Ultimate Penal Sanction*, edited by James R. Acker, Robert M. Bohm, and Charles S. Lanier, 2nd ed. Durham, NC: Duke University Press, 413–468.

Bowers, William, J., Wanda D. Foglia, Jean E. Giles, and Michael E. Antonio. 2006. "The Decision Maker Matters: An Empirical Examination of the Way the Role of the Judge and the Jury

Influence Death Penalty Decision-Making." *Washington and Lee Law Review* 63, no. 3: 931–1010.

Bowers, William J., and Benjamin D. Steiner. 1999. "Death by Default: An Empirical Demonstration of False and Forces Choices in Capital Sentencing." *Texas Law Review* 77, no. 3: 605–717.

Bowers, William J., Benjamin D. Steiner, and Marla Sandys. 2001. "Death Sentencing in Black and White: An Empirical Analysis of the Role of the Juror's Race and Jury Racial Composition." *University of Pennsylvania Journal of Constitutional Law* 3, no. 1: 171–274.

Brewer, Thomas W. 2004. "Race and Jurors' Receptivity to Mitigation in Capital Cases: The Effect of Jurors', Defendants', and Victims' Race in Combination." *Law and Human Behavior* 28: 529–545.

Briggs, Charles. 1986. *Learning How to Ask: A Sociolinguistic Appraisal of the Role of the Interview in Social Science Research.* Cambridge: Cambridge University Press.

Briggs, Charles, and Richard Bauman. 1992. "Genre, Intertextuality, and Social Power." *Journal of Linguistic Anthropology* 2, no. 2: 131–172.

Brooks, Peter, and Paul Gewirtz, eds. 1998. *Law's Stories: Narrative and Rhetoric in the Law.* New Haven: Yale University Press.

Bruner, Jerome. 2008. "Culture and Mind: Their Fruitful Incommensurability." *Ethos* 36, no. 1: 29–45.

Burnett, Ann, and Diane M. Badzinski. 2005. "Judge Nonverbal Communication on Trial: Do Mock Trial Jurors Notice?" *Journal of Communication* 55, no. 2: 209–224.

Burns, Robert, Marianne Constable, Justin Richland, and Winnifred Sullivan. 2008. "Analyzing the Trial: Interdisciplinary Methods." *Political and Legal Anthropology Review* 31, no. 2: 303–329.

Cabana, Donald. 1998. *Death at Midnight: The Confession of an Executioner.* Lebanon, NH: Northeastern University Press.

Caffi, Claudia, and Richard W. Janney. 1994. "Toward a Pragmatics of Emotive Communication." *Journal of Pragmatics* 22, nos. 3–4: 325–373.

Carney, Brian, and Neal Feigenson. 2004. "Visual Persuasion in the Michael Skakel Trial: Enhancing Advocacy through Interactive Media Presentations." *Criminal Justice* 19, no. 1: 22–35.

Carr, Summerson. 2009. "Anticipating and Inhabiting Institutional Identities." *American Ethnologist* 36, no. 2: 317–336.

Carrithers, Michael. 2008. "From Inchoate Pronouns to Proper Nouns: A Theory Fragment with 9/11, Gertrude Stein, and an East German Ethnography." *History and Anthropology* 19, no. 2: 161–186.

Carver, Logan G. 2009. "Single Vote Spares Killer's Life." *Lubbock Avalanche-Journal*, October 8. Retrieved from http://lubbockonline.com/stories/100809/loc_502314885.shtml.

Chen, Rong. 1990. "English Demonstratives: A Case of Semantic Expansion." *Language Sciences* 12, nos. 2–3: 139–153.

Chibundu, Maxwell O. 2006. "Jury Trial and Democratic Values: On the Twenty-First Century Incarnation of an Eighteenth Century Institution." University of Maryland Legal Studies Research Paper 2006–45.

Clay, D. A. 1993. 2007. "Race and Perception in the Courtroom: Nonverbal Behaviors and Attribution in the Criminal Justice System." *Tulane Law Review* 67: 2335–2355.

Coates, Linda, and Allan Wade. 2007. "Language and Violence: Analysis of Four Discursive Operations." *Journal of Family Violence* 22: 511–522.

Cobb, Paul Whitlock, Jr. 1989. "Reviving Mercy in the Structure of Capital Punishment." *Yale Law Journal* 99, no. 2: 389–409.

Cohen, Andrew. 2014. "American Exceptionalism, Crime-and-Punishment Edition." *Atlantic*, February 24. ET. http://www.theatlantic.com/national/archive/2014/02/american-exceptionalism-crime-and-punishment-edition/284021/.

Collier, Richard. 2010. "Masculinities, Law, and Personal Life: Towards a New Framework for Understanding Men, Law, and Gender." *Harvard Journal of Law and Gender* 33, no. 2: 431–475.

Comaroff, John, and Jean Comaroff. 2004. "Criminal Justice, Cultural Justice: The Limits of Liberalism and the Pragmatics of Difference in the New South Africa." *American Ethnologist* 31: 188–204.

Conley, John M. 1980. "Judicial Treatment of Language Variation in American Law." PhD diss., Duke University.

Conley, John M., and William M. O'Barr. 1990. *Rules versus Relationships: The Ethnography of Legal Discourse*. Chicago: University of Chicago Press.

Conley, Robin. 2008. "'At the Time She Was a Man': The Temporal Dimension of Identity Construction." *Political and Legal Anthropology Review* 31, no. 1: 28–47.

Conley, Robin. 2013. "Living with the Decision That Someone Will Die: Linguistic Distance and Empathy in Jurors' Death Penalty Decisions," *Language in Society* 42, no. 5:503–526.

Conley Riner, R. 2017. Discourses of Death: The influence of language on capital jurors' decisions. *Journal of Criminal Justice & Law* 1(1):43-56.

Conley Riner, Robin and Elizabeth Vartkessian. 2018. Communicating Humanity: How defense attorneys use mitigation narratives to advocate for clients. In Avineri, N. et al. (eds). *Language and Social Justice in Practice*. New York: Routledge.

Constable, Marianne. 2014. *Our Word Is Our Bond: How Legal Speech Acts*. Stanford, CA: Stanford University Press.

Cornish, Francis. 2001. "'Modal' That as Determiner and Pronoun: The Primacy of the Cognitive-Interactive Dimension." *English Language and Linguistics* 5, no. 2: 297–315.

Corsevski, Ellen W. 1998. "The Physical Side of Linguistic Violence." *Peace Review* 10, no. 4: 513–516.

Cover, Robert M. 1986. "Violence and the Word." *Yale Law Journal* 95: 1601–1629.

Crapanzano, Vincent. 2004. *Imaginative Horizons: An Essay in Literary-Philosophical Anthropology*. Chicago: University of Chicago Press.

Dabbs, Marjorie O. 1992. "Jury Traumatization in High Profile Criminal Trials: A Case for Crisis Debriefing?" *Law and Psychology Review* 16: 201–216.

Dadds, Mark R., Jennifer L. Allen, Bonamy R. Oliver, Nathan Faulkner, Katherine Legge, Caroline Moul, Matthew Woolgar, and Stephen Scott. 2012. "Love, Eye Contact and the Developmental Origins of Empathy v. Psychopathy." *British Journal of Psychiatry* 200, no. 3: 191–196.

Damasio, Antonio. 2009. *Descartes' Error: Emotion, Reason and the Human Brain*. New York: Random House.

Danet, Brenda. 1980. "'Baby' or 'Fetus'?: Language and the Construction of Reality in a Manslaughter Trial." *Semiotica* 32, nos. 3–4: 187–219.

Daniel, E. Valentine. 1996. *Charred Lullabies: Chapters in an Anthropology of Violence*. Princeton, NJ: Princeton University Press.

Darwin, Charles. 1871. *The Descent of Man, and Selection in Relation to Sex*. London: John Murray.

Das, Veena. 2006. *Life and Words: Violence and the Descent into the Ordinary*. Berkeley: University of California Press.

Das, Veena, and Arthur Kleinman. 1997. Introduction. In *Violence and Subjectivity*, edited by Veena Das, Arthur Kleinman, Mamphela Ramphele, and Pamela Reynolds. Durham, NC: Duke University Press, 1–18.

Death Penalty Information Center. 2013. "The Death Penalty in 2013: Year End Report." www.deathpenaltyinfo.org.

DeWalt, Kathleen M., and Billie R. DeWalt. 2002. *Participant Observation: A Guide for Fieldworkers*. Lanham, MD: AltaMira.

D'hondt, Sigurd. 2009. "Good Cops, Bad Cops: Intertextuality, Agency, and Structure in Criminal Trial Discourse." *Research on Language and Social Interaction* 42, no. 3: 249–275.

Dillehay, Ronald C., and Marla R. Sandys. 1996. "Life under *Wainwright v. Witt*: Juror Dispositions and Death Qualification." *Law and Human Behavior* 20: 147–165.

Dixon, R. M. W. 1994. *Ergativity*. New York: Cambridge University Press.

Douglas, Kevin S., David R. Lyon, and James R. P. Ogloff. 1997. "The Impact of Graphic Photographic Evidence on Mock Jurors' Decisions in a Murder Trial: Probative or Prejudicial?" *Law and Human Behavior* 21, no. 5: 485–501.

Dow, David, and Mark Dow, eds. 2002. *Machinery of Death: The Reality of America's Death Penalty Regime*. New York: Routledge.

Dow, Mark. 2002. "'The Line between Us and Them': Interview with Warden Donald Cabana." In *Machinery of Death: The Reality of America's Death Penalty Regime*, edited by David R. Dow and Mark Dow, 175–194. New York: Routledge.

Drew, Paul, and John Heritage, eds. 1993. *Talk at Work: Interaction in Institutional Settings*. Cambridge: Cambridge University Press.

DuBois, John W. 1980. "Beyond Definiteness: The Trace of Identity in Discourse." In *The Pear Stories: Cognitive, Cultural, and Lin-*

guistic Aspects of Narrative Production, edited by Wallace L. Chafe, 203–274. Norwood, NJ: Ablex.

Duncan, Martha Grace. 2002. "'So Young and So Untender': Remorseless Children and the Expectations of the Law." *Columbia Law Review* 102, no. 6: 1469–1526.

Duranti, Alessandro. 1984. "The Social Meaning of Subject Pronouns in Italian Conversation." *Text* 4, no. 4: 277–311.

Duranti, Alessandro. 1994. *From Grammar to Politics: Linguistic Anthropology in a Western Samoan Village*. Berkeley: University of California Press.

Duranti, Alessandro. 1997. *Linguistic Anthropology*. Cambridge: Cambridge University Press.

Duranti, Alessandro. 2001. *Key Terms in Language and Culture*. Malden, MA: Blackwell.

Duranti, Alessandro. 2004. "Agency in Language." In *A Companion to Linguistic Anthropology*, edited by Alessandro Duranti. Malden, MA: Blackwell, 451–473.

Duranti, Alessandro. 2010. "Husserl, Intersubjectivity and Anthropology." *Anthropological Theory* 10, no. 1: 1–20.

Duranti, Alessandro. 2011. "Ethnopragmatics and Beyond: Intentionality and Agency across Languages and Cultures." In *Hybrids, Differences, Visions: On the Study of Culture*, edited by Claudio Baraldi, Andrea Borsari, and Augusto Carli. Aurora, CO: Davies Group, 151–168.

Durkheim, Emile. 1995. *The Elementary Forms of Religious Life*. 1912. Translated by Karen E. Fields. Paris: F. Alcan.

Dzur, Albert W. 2012. *Punishment, Participatory Democracy, and the Jury*. Oxford: Oxford University Press.

Ehlich, Konrad. 1982. "Anaphora and Deixis: Same, Similar, or Different?" In *Speech, Place and Action: Studies in Deixis and Gesture*, edited by Robert J. Jarvella and Wolfgang Klein, 315–338. Chichester: John Wiley.

Ehrlich, Susan. 2001. *Representing Rape: Language and Sexual Consent*. London: Routledge.

Eisenberg, Theodore, Stephen P. Garvey, and Martin T. Wells. 1996. "Jury Responsibility in Capital Sentencing: An Empirical Study." *Buffalo Law Review* 44: 339–380.

Eisenberg, Theodore, Stephen P. Garvey, and Martin T. Wells. 1998. "But Was He Sorry? The Role of Remorse in Capital Sentencing." *Cornell Law Review* 83: 1599–1637.

Eisenberg, Theodore, and Martin T. Wells. 1993. "Deadly Confusion: Juror Instructions in Capital Cases." *Cornell Law Review* 79: 1–17.

Emily, Jennifer. 2010. "Man Sentenced to Death in 1984 Murder, Rape of SMU Student." *Dallas Morning News*, June 18. http://www.dallasnews.com/news/community-news/dallas/headlines/20100618-Man-sentenced-to-death-in-1984-8811.ece.

Ekman, Paul. 1993. "Facial Expression and Emotion." *American Psychologist* 48, no. 4: 384–392.

Enfield, Nicholas J., and Stephen C. Levinson. 2006. *Roots of Human Sociality: Culture, Cognition and Interaction*. Oxford: Berg.

Fairclough, Norman. 1989. *Language and Power*. Essex: Addison Wesley Longman.

Feigenson, Neal, and Jaihyun Park. 2006. "Emotions and Attributions of Legal Responsibility and Blame: A Research Review." *Law and Human Behavior* 30, no. 2: 143–161.

Feldman, Robert S., and Richard B. Chesley. 1984. "Who Is Lying, Who Is Not: An Attributional Analysis of the Effects of Nonverbal Behavior on Judgements of Defendant Believability." *Behavioral Sciences and the Law* 2, no. 4: 451–461.

Felstiner, William L. F., Richard L. Abel, and Austin Sarat. 1980–1981. "The Emergence and Transformation of Disputes: Naming, Blaming, Claiming . . ." *Law and Society Review* 15, nos. 3–4: 631–654.

Feshbach, Norma D., and Kiki Roe. 1968. "Empathy in Six- and Seven-Year-Olds." *Child Development* 39, no. 1: 133–145.

Fillmore, Charles. 1982. "Towards a Descriptive Framework for Spatial Deixis." In *Speech, Place and Action: Studies in Deixis and Gesture*, edited by Robert J. Jarvella and Wolfgang Klein, 31–59. Chichester: John Wiley.

Fishfader, Vicki L., Gary N. Howells, Roger C. Katz, and Pamela S. Teresi. 1996. "Evidential and Extralegal Factors in Juror Decisions: Presentation Mode, Retention, and Level of Emotionality." *Law and Human Behavior* 20, no. 5: 565–572.

Fletcher, William A. 2014. "Madison Lecture: Our Broken Death Penalty." *New York University Law Review* 89, no. 3: 805–829.

Fleury-Steiner, Benjamin. 2002. "Narratives of the Death Sentence: Toward a Theory of Legal Narrativity." *Law and Society Review* 36, no. 3: 549–576.

Fleury-Steiner, Benjamin. 2004. *Jurors' Stories of Death: How America's Death Penalty Invests in Inequality.* Ann Arbor: University of Michigan Press.

Forman-Barzilai, Fonna. 2005. "Sympathy in Space(s): Adam Smith on Proximity." *Political Theory* 33, no. 2: 189–217.

Forsyth, William. 1878. *History of Trial by Jury.* New York: Cockcroft.

Foucault, Michel. 1977. *Discipline and Punish: The Birth of the Prison.* Translated by Alan Sheridan. London: Allen Lane, Penguin.

Foucault, Michel. 1984. *The Foucault Reader.* Edited by Paul Rabinow. New York: Pantheon Books.

Fox, Aaron. 2004. *Real Country: Music and Language in Working-Class Culture.* Durham, NC: Duke University Press.

Frank, James, and Brandon K. Applegate. 1998. "Assessing Juror Understanding of Capital Sentencing Instructions." *Crime and Delinquency* 44, no. 3: 412–433.

Freiberg, Arie. 2001. "Affective Versus Effective Justice: Instrumentalism and Emotionalism in Criminal Justice." *Punishment and Society* 3, no. 2: 265–278.

Gallese, Vittorio. 2003. "The Manifold Nature of Interpersonal Relations: The Quest for a Common Mechanism." *Philosophical Transactions of the Royal Society of London B* 358, no. 1431: 517–528.

Garvey, Stephen P. 1996. "'As the Gentle Rain from Heaven': Mercy in Capital Sentencing." *Cornell Law Review* 81, no. 5: 989–1048.

Garvey, Stephen P. 1998. "Aggravation and Mitigation in Capital Cases: What Do Jurors Think?" *Columbia Law Review* 98: 1538–1576.

Garvey, Stephen P. 2000. "The Emotional Economy of Capital Sentencing." *New York University Law Review* 75, no. 1: 26–73.

Geertz, Clifford. 1973. "Thick Description: Toward an Interpretive Theory of Culture." In *The Interpretation of Cultures: Selected Essays*, 3–30. New York, NY: Basic Books.

Geimer, William S., and Jonathan Amsterdam. 1989. "Why Jurors Vote Life or Death: Operative Factors in Ten Florida Death Penalty Trials." *American Journal of Criminal Law* 15: 1–54.

Giddens, Anthony. 1979. *Central Problems in Social Theory: Action, Structure and Contradiction in Social Analysis.* London: Macmillan.

Giddens, Anthony. 1984. *The Constitution of Society: Outline of the Theory of Structuration.* Cambridge: Polity.

Gobert, James J. 1988. "In Search of the Impartial Jury." *Journal of Criminal Law and Criminology* 79, no. 2: 269–327.

Gobodo-Madikizela, Pumla. 2003. *A Human Being Died That Night: A South African Story of Forgiveness.* New York: Houghton Mifflin.

Goffman, Erving. 1959. *The Presentation of Self in Everyday Life.* New York: Anchor.

Goffman, Erving. 1981. "Footing." In *Forms of Talk.* Philadelphia: University of Pennsylvania Press.

Goode, Erich, and Nachman Ben-Yehuda. 1994. *Moral Panics: The Social Construction of Deviance.* Malden, MA: Blackwell.

Goodwin, Charles. 1994. "Professional Vision," *American Anthropologist* 96, no. 3: 606–633.

Goodwin, Charles. 2000. "Action and Embodiment within Situated Human Interaction." *Journal of Pragmatics* 32, no. 10: 1489–1522.

Goodwin, Charles. 2003. "The Body in Action." In *Discourse, the Body, and Identity,* edited by Justine Coupland and Richard Gwyn, 19–42. New York: Palgrave Macmillan.

Gordon, Randy. 2011. D. *Rehumanizing Law: A Theory of Law and Democracy.* Toronto: University of Toronto Press.

Gross, Samuel R., and Phoebe C. Ellsworth. 1994. "Hardening of the Attitudes: Americans' Views on the Death Penalty." *Journal of Social Issues* 50, no. 2: 19–52.

Grossman, Dave. 2004. *On Combat: The Psychology and Physiology of Deadly Conflict in War and in Peace.* Milstadt, IL: PPCT Research Publications.

Grossman, Dave. 2009. *On Killing: The Psychological Cost of Learning to Kill in War and Society.* New York: Back Bay Books.

Gumperz, John J. 1983. "Fact and Inference in Courtroom Testimony." In *Language and Social Identity,* edited by John J. Gumperz, 163–194. Cambridge: Cambridge University Press.

Gundel, Jeanette K., Nancy Hedberg, and Ron Zacharski. 1993. "Cognitive Status and the Form of Referring Expressions in Discourse." *Language* 69, no. 2: 274–307.

Gruber, M. 2014. Catherine. *"I'm Sorry for What I've Done": The Language of Courtroom Apologies.* Oxford: Oxford University Press.

Haase, Richard F., and Donald T. Tepper. 1972. "Nonverbal Components of Empathic Communication." *Journal of Counseling Psychology* 19, no. 5: 417–424.

Halverson, Andrea M., Mark Hallahan, Allen J. Hart, and Robert Rosenthal. 1997. "Reducing the Biasing Effects of Judges' Nonverbal Behavior with Simplified Jury Instruction." *Journal of Applied Psychology* 82, no. 4: 590–598.

Haney, Craig. 1984. "Examining Death Qualification: Further Analysis of the Process Effect." *Law and Human Behavior* 8: 133–151.

Haney, Craig. 1994. "Comprehending Life and Death Matters: A Preliminary Study of California's Capital Penalty Instructions." *Law and Human Behavior* 18: 223–248.

Haney, Craig. 1997. "Violence and the Capital Jury: Mechanisms of Moral Disengagement and the Impulse to Condemn to Death." *Stanford Law Review* 49, no. 6: 1447–1486.

Haney, Craig. 2003. "Mental Health Issues in Long-Term Solitary and 'Supermax' Confinement." *Crime and Delinquency* 49, no. 1: 124–156.

Haney, Craig. 2004. "Condemning the Other in Death Penalty Trials: Biographical Racism, Structural Mitigation, and the Empathic Divide." *DePaul Law Review* 53, no. 4: 1557–1589.

Haney, Craig, Lorelei Sontag, and Sally Costanzo. 1994. "Deciding to Take a Life: Capital Juries, Sentencing Instructions, and the Jurisprudence of Death." *Journal of Social Issues* 50, no. 2: 149–176.

Hanks, William F. *Referential Practice.* Chicago: University of Chicago Press, 1990.

Hanks, William F. 2005. "Explorations in the Deictic Field." *Current Anthropology* 46, no. 2: 191–220.

Hanks, William F. 2005. "Pierre Bourdieu and the Practices of Language." *Annual Review of Anthropology* 34: 67–83.

Hansen, Thomas Blom, and Finn Stepputat. 2006. "Sovereignty Revisited." *Annual Review of Anthropology* 35: 295–315.

Haritos-Fatouros, Mika. 2002. *Psychological Origins of Institutionalized Torture.* London: Routledge.

Hatab, Lawrence J. 2002. "Heidegger and the Question of Empathy." In *Heidegger and Practical Philosophy*, edited by François Raffoul and David Pettigrew, 249–274. Albany: State University of New York Press.

Haverkate, Henk. 1992. "Deictic Categories as Mitigating Devices." *Pragmatics* 2, no. 4: 505–522.

Haviland, John B. 1989. "'Sure, Sure': Evidence and Affect." *Text* 9, no. 1: 27–68.

Haviland, John B. 2007. "Person Reference in Tzotzil Gossip: Referring Dupliciter." In *Person Reference in Interaction*, edited by Tanya Stivers and N. J. Enfield, 226–252. Cambridge: Cambridge University Press.

Heidegger, Martin. 1996. *Being and Time: A Translation of Sein und Zeit.* Translated by Joan Stambaugh. Albany: State University of New York Press.

Helion, Chelsea, and David A. Pizarro. 2014. "Beyond Dual-Processes: The Interplay of Reason and Emotion in Moral Judgment." In *Handbook of Neuroethics*, edited by Jens Clausen and Neil Levy. Dordrecht: Springer, 109–125.

Henderson, Lynne. 1987. "Legality and Empathy." *Michigan Law Review* 85: 1574–1653.

Henderson, Lynne. 1988. "The Dialogue of Heart and Head." *Cardozo Law Review* 10, nos. 1–2: 123–148.

Henley, Nancy M., Michelle Miller, and Jo Anne Beazley. 1995. "Syntax, Semantics, and Sexual Violence Agency and the Passive Voice." *Journal of Language and Social Psychology* 14: 60–84.

Hill, Jane. 2008. "Language, Race, and White Public Space." *American Anthropologist* 100, no. 3: 680–689.

Hoffman, Joseph L. 1995. "Where's the Buck: Juror Misperception of Sentencing Responsibility in Death Penalty Cases." *Indiana Law Journal* 70, no. 4: 1137–1160.

Hoffman, Martin L. 1993. "The Contribution of Empathy to Justice and Moral Judgment." In *Readings in Philosophy and Cognitive*

Science, edited by Alvin I. Goldman, 647–680. Cambridge, MA: MIT Press.

Hollan, Douglas. 2001. "Developments in Person-Centered Ethnography." In *The Psychology of Cultural Experience*, edited by Carmella C. Moore and Holly F. Mathews, 48–67. Cambridge: Cambridge University Press.

Hollan, Douglas, and C. Jason Throop. 2008. "What Ever Happened to Empathy? Introduction." *Ethos* 36, no. 4: 385–401.

Hollan, Douglas, and C. Jason Throop. *The Anthropology of Empathy: Experiencing the Lives of Others in Pacific Societies*. New York: Berghahn Books, 2011.

Huggins, Martha K., Mika Haritos-Fatouros, and Philip G. Zimbardo. 2002. *Violence Workers: Police Torturers and Murderers Reconstruct Brazilian Atrocities*. Berkeley: University of California Press.

Hume, David. [1751] 1983. *An Enquiry Concerning the Principles of Morals*. Indianapolis, IN: Hackett.

Husserl, Edmund. 1969. *Formal and Transcendental Logic*. Translated by Dorion Cairns. The Hague: Martinus Nijhoff.

Husserl, Edmund. 1989[1913]. *Ideas Pertaining to a Pure Phenomenology and to a Phenomenological Philosophy. Second Book: Studies in the Phenomenology of Constitution*. Translated by Richard Rojcewicz and André Schuwer. Dordrecht: Kluwer Academic Publishers.

Hutchins, Edwin, and Leysia Palen. 1997. "Constructing Meaning from Space, Gesture, and Speech." In *Discourse, Tools and Reasoning: Essays on Situated Cognition*, edited by Lauren B. Resnick, 23–40. Berlin: Springer-Verlag.

Ignatieff, Michael, ed. 2005. *American Exceptionalism and Human Rights*. Princeton, NJ: Princeton University Press.

Irvine, Judith. 1989. "When Talk Isn't Cheap: Language and Political Economy." *American Ethnologist* 16, no. 2: 248–267.

Jackendoff, Ray. 1972. *Semantic Interpretation in Generative Grammar*. Cambridge, MA: MIT Press.

Jackendoff, Ray. 1990. *Semantic Structures*. Cambridge: MIT Press.

Jackson, Matthew. 2009. "Victim's Husband Gives Testimony at Inmate Trial." *Huntsville Item*. Huntsville, TX, November 13.

http://www.itemonline.com/local/x546208862/Victim-s-husband-gives-testimony-at-inmate-trial?zc_p=0.

Jakobson, Roman. 1990. *On Language*. Edited by Linda R. Waugh and Monique Monville-Burston. Cambridge, MA: Harvard University Press.

"Jury Decides Cop Killer's Punishment." 2008. *KTRK-TV*. ABC. Houston, TX, May 21. http://abclocal.go.com/story?section=news/local&id=6154374.

Keane, Webb. 2002. "Sincerity, 'Modernity,' and the Protestants." *Cultural Anthropology* 17, no. 1: 65–92.

Kerr, Norbert L., Keith E. Niedermeier, and Martin F. Kaplan. 1999. "Bias in Jurors vs. Juries: New Evidence from the SDS Perspective." *Organizational Behavior and Human Decision Processes* 80: 70–86.

Konradi, Amanda. 1999. "'I Don't Have to Be Afraid of You': Rape Survivors' Emotion Management in Court." *Symbolic Interaction* 22, no. 1: 45–77.

Krause, Sharon R. 2011. "Empathy, Democratic Politics, and the Impartial Juror." *Law, Culture and the Humanities* 7: 81–100.

Krebs, Dennis L. 1970. "Altruism: An Examination of the Concept and a Review of the Literature." *Psychological Bulletin* 73, no. 4: 258–302.

LaFrance, Marianne, and Eugene Hahn. 1994. "The Disappearing Agent: Gender Stereotypes, Interpersonal Verbs and Implicit Causality." In *The Women and Language Debate: A Sourcebook*, edited by Camille Roman, Suzanne Juhasz, and Cristanne Miller, 348–362. New Brunswick, NJ: Rutgers University Press.

Lakoff, George. 2009. "Empathy, Sotomayor, and Democracy: The Conservative Stealth Strategy." *Huffington Post*, May 30. http://www.huffingtonpost.com/george-lakoff/empathy-sotomayor-and-dem_b_209406.html.

Lakoff, Robin. 1974. "Remarks on This and That." Paper presented at the Tenth Regional meeting of the Chicago Linguistic Society, Chicago, April 19–21.

Landsman, Stephan. 2002. "Of Mushrooms and Nullifiers: Rules of Evidence and the American Jury." *St. Louis University Public Law Review* 21: 65–83.

Lanier, Charles S., William J. Bowers, and James R. Acker, eds. 2009. *The Future of America's Death Penalty: An Agenda for the Next Generation of Capital Punishment Research*. Durham, NC: Carolina Academic Press.

Laster, Kathy, and Pat O'Malley. 1996. "Sensitive New-Age Laws: The Reassertion of Emotionality in Law." *International Journal of the Sociology of Law* 24, no. 1: 21–40.

Lazarus-Black, Mindie, and Susan F. Hirsch, eds. 1994. *Contested States: Law, Hegemony and Resistance*. New York: Routledge.

Leib, Ethan J. 2008. "A Comparison of Criminal Jury Decision Rules in Democratic Countries." *Ohio State Journal of Criminal Law* 5: 629–644.

Lerner, Jennifer S., and Dacher Keltner. 2000. "Beyond Valence: Toward a Model of Emotion-Specific Influences on Judgment and Choice." *Cognition and Emotion* 14, no. 4: 473–493.

Lerner, Jennifer S., and Dacher Keltner. 2001. "Fear, Anger, and Risk." *Journal of Personality and Social Psychology* 81, no. 1: 146–159.

LeVan, Elizabeth A. 1984. "Nonverbal Communication in the Courtroom: Attorney Beware." *Law and Psychology Review* 8: 83–104.

Levenson, Laurie L. 2008. "Courtroom Demeanor: The Theater of the Courtroom." *Minnesota Law Review* 92: 573–633.

Levinas, Emmanuel. 1969. *Totality and Infinity: An Essay on Exteriority*. Pittsburgh, PA: Duquesne University Press.

Levinas, Emmanuel. 1985. *Ethics and Infinity: Conversations with Philippe Nemo*. Translated by Richard A. Cohen. Pittsburgh: Duquesne University Press.

LeVine, Robert. 1982. *Culture, Behavior, and Personality*. New Brunswick, NJ: Rutgers University Press.

Levinson, Stephen C. 1983. "Deixis." In *Pragmatics*. Cambridge: Cambridge University Press, 54–96.

Linder, Douglas. 1996. "Juror Empathy and Race." *Tennessee Law Review* 63: 887–916.

Llewellyn, Karl N., and E. Adamson Hoebel. 1941. *The Cheyenne Way: Conflict and Case Law in Primitive Jurisprudence*. Norman: University of Oklahoma Press.

Loewenstein, George, and Deborah A. Small. 2007. "The Scarecrow and the Tin Man: The Vicissitudes of Human Sympathy and Caring." *Review of General Psychology* 11, no. 2: 112–126.

Luginbuhl, James, and Julie Howe. 1995. "Discretion in Capital Sentencing Instructions: Guided or Misguided?" *Indiana Law Journal* 70, no. 4: 1161–1181.

Lutz, Catherine, and Geoffrey M. White. 1986. "The Anthropology of Emotions." *Annual Review of Anthropology* 15: 405–436.

Lynch, Mona. 2000. "On-line Executions: The Symbolic Use of the Electric Chair in Cyberspace." *Political and Legal Anthropology Review* 23, no. 2: 1–20.

Lynch, Mona. 2002. "Pedophiles and Cyber-predators as Contaminating Forces: The Language of Disgust, Pollution, and Boundary Invasions in Federal Debates on Sex Offender Legislation." *Law and Social Inquiry* 27, no. 3: 529–566.

Lynch, Mona, and Craig Haney. 2000. "Discrimination and Instructional Comprehension: Guided Discretion, Racial Bias, and the Death Penalty." *Law and Human Behavior* 24, no. 3: 337–358.

Lynch, Mona, and Craig Haney. 2009. "Capital Jury Deliberation: Effects on Death Sentencing, Comprehension, and Discrimination." *Law and Human Behavior* 33, no. 6: 481–496.

Lynch, Mona, and Craig Haney. 2011a. "Looking across the Empathic Divide: Racialized Decision Making on the Capital Jury." *Michigan State Law Review* 2011: 573–607.

Lynch, Mona, and Craig Haney. 2011b. "Mapping the Racial Bias of the White Male Capital Juror: Jury Composition and the 'Empathic Divide.'" *Law and Society Review* 45, no. 1: 69–102.

Lyons, John. 1977. *Semantics.* 2 vols. Cambridge: Cambridge University Press.

Lyons, John. 1982. "Deixis and Subjectivity: Loquor, ergo sum?" In *Speech, Place and Action: Studies in Deixis and Gesture,* edited by Robert J. Jarvella and Wolfgang Klein. Chichester: John Wiley, 101–124.

MacKinnon, Catherine. 1993. *Only Words.* Cambridge, MA: Harvard University Press.

Madeira, Jody Lynee. 2012. *Killing McVeigh: The Death Penalty and the Myth of Closure.* New York: New York University Press.

Malinowski, Bronislaw. 1935. *Coral Gardens and Their Magic: A Study of the Methods of Tilling the Soil and of Agricultural Rites in the Trobriand Islands.* London: Routledge.

Manzo, John. 1996. "Taking Turns and Taking Sides: Opening Scenes from Two Jury Deliberations." *Social Psychology Quarterly* 59, no. 2: 107–125.

Marcus, George. *The Sentimental Citizen: Emotion in Democratic Politics.* University Park: Penn State University Press, 2002.

Markkanen, Raija, and Hartmut Schröder, eds. 1997. *Hedging and Discourse: Approaches to the Analysis of a Pragmatic Phenomenon.* Berlin: de Gruyter.

Maroney, Terry A. 2006. "Law and Emotion: A Proposed Taxonomy of an Emerging Field." *Law and Hum Behavior* 30: 119–142.

Martinez, Samuel. 2009. *International Migration and Human Rights: The Global Repercussions of U.S. Policy.* Berkeley: University of California Press.

Massey, Doreen. 2005. *For Space.* London: Sage.

Matlon, Ronald J. 1988. *Communication in the Legal Process.* New York: Holt, Rinehart and Winston.

Matoesian, Gregory M. 2008a. "You Might Win the Battle but Lose the War: Multimodal, Interactive and Extralinguistic Aspects of Witness Resistance." *Journal of English Linguistics* 36, no. 3: 195–219.

Matoesian, Gregory M. 2008b. "Role Conflict as an Interactional Resource in the Multimodal Emergence of Expert Identity." *Semiotica* 171: 15–49.

McAdams, John. 1998. "Racial Disparity and the Death Penalty." *Law and Contemporary Problems* 61: 153.

McClanahan, Jon P. 2009. "The 'True' Right to Trial by Jury: The Founders' Formulation and Its Demise." *West Virginia Law Review* 111: 791–830.

Mertz, Elizabeth. "Legal Language: Pragmatics, Poetics, and Social Power." *Annual Review of Anthropology* 23 (1994): 435–455.

Mertz, Elizabeth. 2007. *The Language of Law School: Learning to "Think Like a Lawyer."* New York: Oxford University Press.

Milgram, Stanley. 1974. *Obedience to Authority: An Experimental View.* New York: Harper & Row.

Miller, Monica K., and R. David Hayward. "Religious Characteristics and the Death Penalty." *Law and Human Behavior* 32: 113–123.

Mulcahy, Linda. 2007. "Architects of Justice: The Politics of Courtroom Design." *Social and Legal Studies* 16, no. 3: 383–403.

Mustard, David B. 2001. "Racial, Ethnic, and Gender Disparities in Sentencing: Evidence from the U.S. Federal Courts." Journal of Law and Economics 44, no. 1: 285–314.

Nussbaum, Martha C. 1996. "Emotion in the Language of Judging." *St. John's Law Review* 70, no. 1: 23–30.

Nussbaum, Martha C. 1999. "'Secret Sewers of Vice': Disgust, Bodies, and the Law." In *The Passions of Law*, edited by Susan A. Bandes, 19–62. New York: New York University Press.

Nussbaum, Martha C. 2004. *Hiding from Humanity: Disgust, Shame, and the Law*. Princeton, NJ: Princeton University Press.

Ochs, Elinor. 2002. "Becoming a Speaker of Culture." In *Language Acquisition and Language Socialization: Ecological Perspectives*, edited by Claire Kramsch, 99–120. New York: Continuum.

Ochs, Elinor. 2012. "Experiencing Language." *Anthropological Theory* 12, no. 2: 142–160.

Ochs, Elinor, and Lisa Capps. 1995. *Constructing Panic: The Discourse of Agoraphobia*. Cambridge, MA: Harvard University Press.

Ochs, Elinor, and Olga Solomon. 2010. "Autistic Sociality." *Ethos* 38, no. 1: 69–92.

Ortner, Sherry. 2006. *Anthropology and Social Theory: Culture, Power, and the Acting Subject*. Durham, NC: Duke University Press.

Osofsky, Michael J., Albert Bandura, and Philip G. Zimbardo. 2005. "The Role of Moral Disengagement in the Execution Process." *Law and Human Behavior* 29, no. 4: 371–393.

Ostman, Jan-Ola. 1995. "Recasting the Deictic Foundation, Using Physics and Finnish." In *Essays in Semantics and Pragmatics*, edited by Masayoshi Shibatani and Sandra A. Thompson, 247–278. Amsterdam: John Benjamins.

Otterbein, Keith F. 1988. *The Ultimate Coercive Sanction: A Cross-Cultural Study of Capital Punishment*. New Haven: HRAF Press.

Paredes, Américo. 1995. *Folklore and Culture on the Texas-Mexican Border*. Edited by Richard Bauman. Austin: University of Texas Press.

Patterson, Miles L. 1983. *Nonverbal Behavior: A Functional Perspective*. New York: Springer-Verlag.

Pomerantz, Anita. 1984. "Agreeing and Disagreeing with Assessments: Some Features of Preferred and Dispreferred Turn Shapes." In *Structures of Social Action*, edited by J. M. Atkinson and J. Heritage, 57–101. Cambridge: Cambridge University Press.

Pryor, Bert, and Raymond W. Buchanan. 1984. "The Effects of a Defendant's Demeanor on Juror Perceptions of Credibility and Guilt." *Journal of Communication* 34, no. 3: 92–99.

Rabinow, Paul. 1977. *Reflections on Fieldwork in Morocco*. Berkeley: University of California Press.

Rafter, Nicole H. 2006. *Shots in the Mirror: Crime Films and Society*. 2nd ed. New York: Oxford University Press.

Ramos-Zayas, Ana. 2011. "Learning Affect, Embodying Race: Youth, Blackness, and Neoliberal Emotions in Latino Newark." *Transforming Anthropology* 19, no. 2: 86–104.

Regional Public Defenders for Capital Cases. 2012. Lubbock, Texas. rpdo.org.

Remland, Martin S. 1994. "The Importance of Nonverbal Communication in the Courtroom." *New Jersey Journal of Communication* 2, no. 2: 124–145.

Rorty, Amelie Oksenberg. 1995. "Understanding Others." In *Other Intentions: Cultural Contexts and the Attribution of Inner States*, edited by Lawrence Rosen, 203–224. Sante Fe, NM: School of American Research Press.

Rose, Mary R., Shari S. Diamond, and Kimberly M. Baker. 2010. "Goffman on the Jury: Real Jurors' Attention to the 'Offstage' of Trials." *Law and Human Behavior* 34, no. 4: 310–323.

Ryfe, David Michael. 2002. "The Practice of Deliberative Democracy: A Study of 16 Deliberative Organizations." *Political Communication* 19: 359–377.

Rymes, Betsy. 1995. "The Construction of Moral Agency in the Narratives of High-School Drop-Outs." *Discourse and Society* 6, no. 4: 495–516.

Sacks, Harvey, and Emanuel A. Schegloff. 1979. "Two Preferences in the Organization of Reference to Persons in Conversation and Their Interaction." In *Everyday Language: Studies in Ethnomethodology*, edited by George Psathas, 15–21. New York: Irvington.

Saldívar, José David. 1997. *Border Matters: Remapping American Cultural Studies*. Berkeley: University of California Press.

Salekin, Randall T., James R. P. Ogloff, Cathy McFarland, and Richard Rogers. 1995. "Influencing Jurors' Perceptions of Guilt: Expression of Emotionality during Testimony." *Behavioral Sciences and the Law* 13, no. 2: 293–305.

Salgado, Richard. 2005. "Tribunals Organized to Convict: Searching for a Lesser Evil in the Capital Juror Death-Qualification Process in *United States v. Green*." *Brigham Young University Law Review* 2005, no. 2: 519–552.

Sandys, Marla, and Scott McClelland. 2003. "Stacking the Deck for Guilt and Death: The Failure of Death Qualification to Ensure Impartiality." In *America's Experiment with Capital Punishment: Reflections on the Past, Present, and Future of the Ultimate Penal Sanction* 2nd ed., edited by James R. Acker, Robert M. Bohm, and Charles S. Lanier, 385–412. Durham, NC: Carolina Academic Press.

Sarat, Austin. 1995. "Violence, Representation, and Responsibility in Capital Trials: The View from the Jury." *Indiana Law Journal* 70, no. 4: 1103–1135.

Sarat, Austin, 2001a. *The Killing State: Capital Punishment in Law, Politics, and Culture*. Oxford: Oxford University Press.

Sarat, Austin, 2001b. *When the State Kills*. Princeton, NJ: Princeton University Press.

Sarat, Austin. 2005. "Mercy, Clemency, and Capital Punishment: Two Accounts." Schwartz Lecture, Moritz College of Law, Ohio State University, Columbus, April 22.

Sarat, Austin, and Christian Boulanger. 2005. *The Cultural Lives of Capital Punishment*. Stanford, CA: Stanford University Press.

Savitsky, Jeffrey C., and Marguerite E. Sim. 1974. "Trading Emotions: Equity Theory of Reward and Punishment." *Journal of Communication* 24, no. 3: 140–147.

Schegloff, Emanuel A. 1979. "The Relevance of Repair for Syntax-for-Conversation." In *Syntax and Semantics 12: Discourse and*

Syntax, edited by Talmy Givon, 261–288. New York: Academic Press.

Schegloff, Emanuel A. 1996. "Some Practices for Referring to Persons in Talk-in Interaction: A Partial Sketch of a Systematics." In *Studies in Anaphora*, edited by Barbara A. Fox, 437–485. Amsterdam: John Benjamins.

Schegloff, Emanuel A. 2007a. "Categories in Action: Person-Reference and Membership Categorization." *Discourse Studies* 9, no. 4(: 433–461.

Schegloff, Emanuel A. 2007b. "A Tutorial on Membership Categorization." *Journal of Pragmatics* 39: 462–482.

Schieffelin, Bambi, Kathryn Ann Woolard, and Paul V. Kroskrity. 1998. *Language Ideologies: Practice and Theory*. New York: Oxford University Press.

Schiffrin, Deborah. 1994. *Approaches to Discourse*. Malden, MA: Blackwell.

Searcy, Michael, Steve Duck, and Peter Blanck. 2004. "Communication in the Courtroom and the "Appearance" of Justice." In *Nonverbal Behavior in the Courtroom*, edited by Michael Searcy, Steve Duck, and Peter Blanck. Hillsdale, NJ: Lawrence Erlbaum.

Sheyn, Elizabeth R. 2010. "A Foothold for Real Democracy in Eastern Europe." *Vanderbilt Journal of Transnational Law* 43: 649–699.

Sidnell, Jack. 2010. "Conversation Analysis." In *Sociolinguistics and Language Education*, edited by Nancy H. Hornberger and Sandra Lee McKay, 492–527. Bristol: Multilingual Matters.

Singer, Melissa, Joshua Radinsky, and Susan R. Goldman. 2008. "The Role of Gesture in Meaning Construction." *Discourse Processes* 45, nos. 4–5: 365–386.

Smith, Adam. [1759] 1982. *The Theory of Moral Sentiments*. Edited by D. D. Raphael and A. L. Macfie. Indianapolis: Liberty Fund.

Spener, David. 2009. *Clandestine Crossings: Migrants and Coyotes on the Texas-Mexico Border*. Ithaca, NY: Cornell University Press.

Stanley, A. J. 1977. "Who Should Conduct the Voir Dire: The Judge." *Judicature* 61: 70–75.

Steiker, Carol S. 2005. "Capital Punishment and American Exceptionalism." In *American Exceptionalism and Human Rights*, edited by Michael Ignatieff, 57–89. Princeton, NJ: Princeton University Press.

Steiker, Carol S., and Jordan M. Steiker. 1995. "Sober Second Thoughts: Reflections on Two Decades of Constitutional Regulation of Capital Punishment." *Harvard Law Review* 109: 355–438.

Steiker, Carol S., and Jordan M. Steiker. 2013. "*Miller v. Alabama*: Is Death (Still) Different?" *Ohio State Journal of Criminal Law* 11: 37–56.

Stein, Edith. 1989. *On the Problem of Empathy*. 3rd ed. Translated by Waltraut Stein. Washington, DC: ICS Publications.

Stivers, Tanya. 2007. "Alternative Recognitionals in Person Reference." In *Person Reference in Interaction: Linguistic, Cultural, and Social Perspectives*, edited by Nick J. Enfield and Tanya Stivers, 73–96. Cambridge: Cambridge University Press.

Stivers, Tanya, N. J. Enfield, and Stephen C. Levinson. 2007. "Person Reference in Interaction." In *Person Reference in Interaction: Linguistic, Cultural, and Social Perspectives*, edited by N. J. Enfield and Tanya Stivers, 1–20. Cambridge: Cambridge University Press.

Strauss, Claudia. 2004. "Is Empathy Gendered and, If So, Why? An Approach from Feminist Psychological Anthropology." *Ethos* 32, no. 4: 432–457.

Strauss, Susan. 2002. "This, That, and It in Spoken American English: A Demonstrative System of Gradient Focus." *Language Sciences* 24, no. 2: 131–152.

Streeck, Jürgen. 2003. "The Body Taken for Granted: Lingering Dualism in Research on Social Interaction." In *Studies in Language and Social Interaction: In Honor of Robert Hopper*, edited by Phillip J. Glenn, Curtis D. LeBaron, and Jenny Mandelbaum, 366–376. Mahwah, NJ: Lawrence Erlbaum.

Streeck, Jürgen, Charles Goodwin, and Curtis D. LeBaron, eds. 2014. *Embodied Interaction: Language and Body in the Material World*. Cambridge: Cambridge University Press.

Sundby, Scott E. 1997. "Capital Jury and Absolution: The Intersection of Trial Strategy, Remorse and the Death Penalty." *Cornell Law Review* 83: 1557–1598.

Sundby, Scott E. 2005. *A Life and Death Decision: A Jury Weighs the Death Penalty.* New York: Palgrave Macmillan.

Sween, Gretchen. 2014. "Texas Ain't Tuscany: How a Truism Might Further Invigorate Contemporary 'Cost Argument' for Death Penalty Abolition." *American Journal of Criminal Law* 41, no. 2: 151–189.

Swierzbin, Bonnie. 2010. "'Demonstratives' Special Place in the English Reference System: Why *That*'s Important for English Language Learners." *Language and Linguistics Compass* 4, no. 10: 987–1000.

Tamanaha, Brian Z. 2004. *On the Rule of Law: History, Politics, Theory.* Cambridge: Cambridge University Press.

Texas Defender Service. 2004. *Deadly Speculation: Misleading Texas Capital Juries with False Predictions of Future Dangerousness.* Houston: Texas Defender Service.

Throop, C. Jason. 2008. "On the Problem of Empathy: The Case of Yap, Federated States of Micronesia." *Ethos* 36, no. 4: 402–426.

Throop, C. Jason. 2010. "Latitudes of Loss: On the Vicissitudes of Empathy." *American Ethnologist* 37, no. 4: 771–782.

Trager, George L. 1958. "Paralanguage: A First Approximation." *Studies in Linguistics* 13: 1–12.

Tsoudis, Olga. 2002. "The Influence of Empathy in Mock Jury Criminal Cases: Adding to the Affect Control Model." *Western Criminology Review* 4, no. 1: 55–67.

Unnever, James, and Francis T. Cullen. 2007. "Reassessing the Racial Divide in Support for Capital Punishment: The Continuing Significance of Race." *Journal of Research in Crime and Delinquency* 44: 124–158.

Vartkessian, Elizabeth, Jon R. Sorensen, and Christopher E. Kelly. 2014. "Tinkering with the Machinery of Death: An Analysis of Juror Decision-Making in Texas Death Penalty Trials during Two Statutory Eras." *Justice Quarterly*, September 24, 1–24.

Vidmar, Neil, and Valerie P. 1986. Hans. *Judging the Jury.* New York: Plenum Press.

Vidmar, Neil, and Valerie P. 2007. Hans. *American Juries: The Verdict.* Amherst, NY: Prometheus Books.

Waller, James. 2002. *Becoming Evil: How Ordinary People Commit Genocide and Mass Killing*. New York: Oxford.

Weisberg, Robert. 1983. "Deregulating Death." *Supreme Court Review* 1983: 305–395.

Wiener, Richard L., Brian H. Bornstein, and Amy Voss. 2006. "Emotion and the Law: A Framework for Inquiry." *Law and Human Behavior* 30, no. 2: 231–248.

Wiener, Richard L., Michael Holtje, Ryan J. Winter, Jason A. Cantone, Susan Block-Lieb, and Karen Gross. 2006. "Psychology and BAPCPA: Enhanced Disclosure and Emotion." *Missouri Law Review* 71, no. 4: 1003–1033.

Weiner, Richard L., Melanie Rogers, Ryan Winter, Linda Hurt, Amy Hackney, Karen Kadela, Hope Seib, Shannon Rauch, Laura Warren, and Ben Morasco. 2004. "Guided Jury Discretion in Capital Murder Cases." *Psychology, Public Policy, and Law* 10, no. 4: 516–576.

Williams, Paige. 2014. "Witnesses to a Botched Execution." *New Yorker*, April 30. http://www.newyorker.com/news/news-desk/witnesses-to-a-botched-execution.

Wispé, Lauren. 1986. "The Distinction between Sympathy and Empathy: To Call Forth a Concept, a Word Is Needed." *Journal of Personality and Social Psychology* 50, no. 2: 314–321.

Wispé, Lauren. 1991. *The Psychology of Sympathy*. New York: Plenum Press.

Wogan, Peter. 2004. "Deep Hanging Out: Reflections on Fieldwork and Multisited Andean Ethnography." *Identities: Global Studies in Culture and Power* 11, no. 1: 129–139.

Zacharias, Fred C. 2004. "Lawyers as Gatekeepers." *San Diego Law Review* 41: 1387–1405.

Zigon, Jarrett. 2007. "Moral Breakdown and the Ethical Demand: A Theoretical Framework for an Anthropology of Moralities." *Anthropological Theory* 7, no. 2: 131–150.

Cases Cited

Batson v. Kentucky, 476 U.S. 79 (1986)

Caldwell v. Mississippi, 472 U.S. 320 (1985)

Callins v. Collins, 510 U.S. 1141 (1994)

Carey v. Musladin 549 U.S. 70 (2006)

Estelle v. Williams 425 u.s. 501 (1976)

Furman v. Georgia, 408 U.S. 238 (1972)

Gregg v. Georgia, 428 U.S. 153 (1976)

Holbrook v. Flynn 475 U.S. 560 (1986)

Jurek v. Texas, 428 U.S. 262 (1976)

Kovacs v. Szentes, 130 Conn. 229 (1943)

McGautha v. California, 302 U.S. 183 (1971)

McKlesky v.Kemp, 481 U.S. 279 (1987)

Mills v.Maryland, 486 U.S. 367 (1988)

Morgan v. Illinois, 594 U.S. 719 (1992)

Penry v. Lynaugh, 492 U.S. 302 (1989)

Proffit v. Florida, 428 U.S. 242 (1976)

Strauder v. West Virginia, 100 U.S. 303 (1980)

Woodson v. North Carolina, 428 U.S. 280 (1976)

INDEX

CPSIA information can be obtained
at www.ICGtesting.com
Printed in the USA
BVHW071521221220
596060BV00004B/10